Responsibility

PHILOSOPHY OF EDUCATION IN PRACTICE

SERIES EDITORS: MARIT HONERØD HOVEID, IAN MUNDAY AND AMY SHUFFELTON

This series of short form books explores issues, topics and themes that are foundational to educational practices both within and beyond the boundaries of formal education. With books on topics such as collaboration, responsibility, touch and emotions, the series generates philosophical discussions of education that are accessible to the curious reader and draws out commonalities and differences in thinking about and doing education across cultures. By addressing educational thought and practice in a philosophical manner the series encourages us to look beyond pre-specified 'learning outcomes' and asks us to slow down and explore the messiness and complexity of educational situations.

ADVISORY BOARD:

ALSO AVAILABLE IN THE SERIES:

Collaboration, Amy Shuffelton

FORTHCOMING IN THE SERIES:

Emotions, Liz Jackson

Responsibility

Philosophy of Education in Practice

BARBARA S. STENGEL

BLOOMSBURY ACADEMIC
LONDON • NEW YORK • OXFORD • NEW DELHI • SYDNEY

BLOOMSBURY ACADEMIC
Bloomsbury Publishing Plc
50 Bedford Square, London, WC1B 3DP, UK
1385 Broadway, New York, NY 10018, USA
29 Earlsfort Terrace, Dublin 2, Ireland

BLOOMSBURY, BLOOMSBURY ACADEMIC and the Diana logo are trademarks of Bloomsbury Publishing Plc

First published in Great Britain 2024

Series design by Grace Ridge
Cover illustration © Tyas drawing / iStock

A catalogue record for this book is available from the British Library.

A catalog record for this book is available from the Library of Congress.

ISBN: HB: 978-1-3503-0260-0
PB: 978-1-3503-0261-7
ePDF: 978-1-3503-0259-4
eBook: 978-1-3503-0262-4

Series: Philosophy of Education in Practice

Typeset by Deanta Global Publishing Services, Chennai, India
Printed and bound in Great Britain

To Henry, Will, Maggie, Fran, and Lucy, my next generation,
for whom developing responsibility is the challenge

CONTENTS

SERIES EDITORS' FOREWORD

Responsibility is the second book in the series Philosophy of Education in Practice. It is a common enough experience for both educators and those being educated, to find themselves bamboozled, bothered, or discombobulated by the kinds of things that happen during educational encounters and settings. Trying to understand such experiences and acknowledge their meaning and import is something that can nag away at us. We hope that readers who are drawn toward exploring such concerns will find this book and the series to which it belongs, helpful in developing a deeper and more nuanced understanding of educational practice. Addressing educational thought and practice in a philosophical manner takes us beyond the sanctuary of pre-specified "learning outcomes" and asks us to slow down and explore the messiness and complexity of educational situations.

This series aims to explore the connections between thinking and doing in education through a variety of philosophical lenses. Authors will address diverse issues, topics, and themes, in multiple contexts, from a variety of perspectives. Throughout this series, we hope to elucidate the commonalities and differences in thinking and doing education across and between cultures. What holds the series together is not a particular point of view but instead a shared emphasis and approach. Each book will connect experiences (doing) and enduring questions in philosophy of education (thinking) to explore a major concept in education. Recent philosophical work has not shirked a concern with educational virtues and values, but its treatment of these matters is sometimes narrowly academic. We believe that educators, administrators, policy professionals, parents, and other citizens curious about education would benefit from a broadly accessible, yet rich, treatment that offers fresh perspectives on enduring dimensions of education. While the series is designed to speak to practitioners, who are interested in reading theoretical work, the books in this series are not intended as "how to" guides — we would not presume to lecture to those working in the field, or attempt to find hard and fast solutions to educational problems. Rather, the authors in the series aim to philosophically inhabit practice and offer meditations on alternative ways of thinking/doing which arise from their research or teaching within the current neoliberal, globalized context.

SERIES EDITORS'

Marit Honerød Hoveid
Ian Munday
Amy Shuffelton

Volume Two: Responsibility

In the second volume of the series, Barbara Stengel explores the theme of "responsibility" by reflecting on her role as a critical friend to the new Principal of Bailey STEM Magnet Middle School in Nashville, Tennessee. At the time of his appointment, the school in question was home to a cohort of students hailing from some of the most disadvantaged communities in the city. It was the worst-performing middle school in Tennessee. For Stengel, attempts by the principal and staff at Bailey to turn around the fortunes of the school provide an exemplary case of educational responsibility. Here, "responsibility" is conceived of in terms of response-ability—the capacity to respond fruitfully and fittingly to challenging situations and to the persons involved. Through the use of vivid examples, Stengel shows how the response-ability practiced at Bailey had edu-political, pedagogical, and personal dimensions. One aspect of the book which is sure to strike readers is the way in which "responsibility" is counterpoised with a more popular and ubiquitous term in schooling, namely, "accountability." Indeed, in stark terms, Stengel shows how the practices and modes of thought associated with the former shed light on the damaging limitations of the latter. In her account of what happened at Bailey, she shows how attentiveness to the expressed needs of students and staff can have powerful consequences which surpass the rigorous adherence to state directives and one-size fits all conceptions of best practice. Stengel offers readers some surprising and creative approaches to solving educational problems that are, if not always as drastic as those facing Bailey, constant and widespread.

Though deeply rooted in the specifics of a particular context, *Responsibility* has a rich international dimension. Stengel draws on a variety of philosophical traditions to explore "responsibility" including critical pragmatism, existentialism, and moral realism. Moreover, this book has broad applicability. Readers are invited to consider ways in which the particularities of their own schooling contexts may be addressed by responsibly agile moves which swerve and skip away from the deadening grip of accountability culture. Such moves are clearly on display in Stengel's engrossing and touching account of a school which attempted to do just that.

ACKNOWLEDGMENTS

Ideas inhabit our lives in remarkable ways. Responsibility has followed me around my entire life. As the oldest daughter of Anne and Walter Senkowski in Philadelphia in the 1950s and 1960s, responsibility was a constant companion. As a student in Catholic schools from 1958 through 1970, I was never far from a reminder about my responsibility. Blessedly, the adults in my life at that time understood deeply the point that I make in this book: that the experience of response-ability is the path to legitimate responsibility and that a capacity for response flourishes when one is secure and cared for. I am forever grateful to my parents and also to Pat Wallace, Sr. M. St. Irminus, IHM, and other educators for knowing this and making it real for me. Because of their wisdom and understanding, I was able to grow in responsibility while avoiding the accountability-induced neuroses of the Catholic school girl.

It is no accident then that I paid attention in 1976 when Sr. Kathleen Toner, IHM introduced me to H. R. Niebuhr's *The Responsible Self* when I was a master's student in religious studies at Catholic University. It was also at Catholic University that I first encountered the philosophy and ethical theory of John Dewey, though it would be David Engel at the University of Pittsburgh whose dual role as an educational philosopher and a school board president helped me to appreciate what a pragmatist perspective could offer educational practice. Philosopher Wilfred Sellars showed me that pragmatism was everywhere, even when it masqueraded in analytic dot quotes. The mark of these educator-philosophers can be seen in this work.

Over the intervening years, I have been challenged and inspired by innumerable students and colleagues in teacher education and philosophy at Millersville University in Pennsylvania and Peabody College, Vanderbilt University, to get clearer on what difference response-ability might make. Beginning in 1999, I presented papers and participated in symposia that explored response-ability and its link to responsibility in the ethics of educational practice. Those papers prompted innumerable conversations with colleagues that have shaped the present work, and one lengthy collaboration — with Alan Tom — on the ethics of teaching that kept my attention on *Moral Matters* for years.

In recent months, Deborah Kerdeman, Marcy Singer-Gabella, Nadav Ehrenfeld, Grace Chen, Michael Neel, Deron Boyles, Becky Peterson, and Liz Self offered, sometimes unknowingly, important insights and suggestions on this text and the ideas it develops. This book is better because of their shared wisdom. And I have much appreciated Monica Starrett's regular reminders to me over the past decade that response, responsiveness, and responsibility map the entry to response-ability.

As this manuscript became a book, Marit Honerød Hoveid, Amy Shuffelton, and Ian Munday (the Series Editors) and at least one not-so-anonymous reviewer offered both substantial encouragement and pointed criticism on my proposal and a penultimate draft. Both enabled me to write a better book and submit the final version only a little later than I promised it!

Most of all, I have been inspired and challenged by parenting two children who have become marvelous adults, Tim Stengel and Emily Lyons. This is what response-ability looks like.

I am delighted to surrender responsibility now to Dr. Christian Sawyer, Dr. Claire Jasper-Crafter, and the Bailey team who made my work on this project possible and who have so impressed me with their capacity to respond with care and intelligence to every educational situation they faced with critical consciousness, attention to relation, and openness to uncertainty.

Each of the persons named here deserves my acknowledgment. That acknowledgment comes with my love and thanks.

CHAPTER 1

Introduction

For four years, from 2012 to 2016, I spent one full day a week at Bailey STEM Magnet Middle School in Nashville, Tennessee. To be a middle school in Nashville is to educate fifth through eighth graders in one building. To be a STEM school is to build a curricular program that has science, technology, and mathematics at its core. To be a Magnet School situates Bailey in the domain of "choice" in the American system; families who live outside of a school's attendance zone can choose to send their student to a school so designated. But Bailey was a school of choice that few families and students chose.

As our story begins (in July of 2012), Bailey was known to be the worst middle school in the state of Tennessee—by local reputation and by state rankings. The school was the educational home of many of the most disadvantaged children in Nashville. The brick building that housed Bailey's 400+ students was large, sprawling, and impressive even, but riddled with mechanical systems that had seen better days and far less attention to upkeep than was needed. The predominantly Black student body came to school every day on buses that traversed rapidly gentrifying neighborhoods in East Nashville, neighborhoods that had already become largely white and increasingly wealthy. The students were not wanted in that space. Had the school vaporized on the spot in 2012, nobody—not even the families served there—would have grieved.

I wasn't at Bailey to study responsibility. I was there to enact my own response-ability as an educator preparing teachers for a system that has lost its way and continues to discriminate against poor students of color. I was also there as the director of a residency program, as a lead instructor in a district-university masters' degree partnership, and as a "critical friend" to a brand-new principal. That I learned more than I taught will surprise no one who has tried to work across schools and universities. That I saw responsibility everywhere I looked, everywhere I interacted, may give you pause. As I began this book project, near the end of a long career of thinking about responsibility in response-ability terms, that is, as the capacity to respond fruitfully and fittingly to challenging situations, my Bailey experience loomed large as you shall see. Think with me for a moment about examples of edu-political, pedagogical, and personal response-ability.

Variations on Response-ability

Edu-political Response-ability

When new executive principal Dr. Christian Sawyer[1] arrived at Bailey STEM Magnet Middle School for the first time, he encountered a generally poor and mostly Black student population and a staff of teachers who were skeptical about what could be done to increase student achievement (just 12 percent of students scored Proficient on state tests) or to improve student well-being (in a school designated by the state as "persistently dangerous"). What Sawyer had going for him was that he paid close and responsive attention to the talent of the students and the support of the teachers. This may sound like an obvious expectation of a person taking up this role, but too often, students and teachers get lost in the shuffle of administrative constraints.

What that attention told him was that business as usual wasn't going to result in the growth and development of young people who were systematically disadvantaged.

Bailey was, as teacher leader Whitney Bradley noted, "a Black school run by white people." There were no people of color in positions of leadership. Even as Principal Sawyer shook every scholar's hand as they entered the building in the morning—and referred to them unfailingly as "scholars," the students did not know how to interpret this new situation (a white man replacing a Black woman as principal) or how to respond in their own best interests.

Before fall turned to winter, Sawyer realized that he needed to change gears. He came to my house for a spaghetti dinner and a little free advice. He had ideas—about teacher leaders and teams and culturally relevant and sustaining pedagogies. He knew that teachers' ideas and commitments had to be honored and teachers' bodies and souls cared for; he knew that teaching is a team sport; he knew that instruction had to interest students, but also that it needed to be targeted for individuals and small groups in order to personalize learning and overcome what today we would call "learning loss." He knew that consistent and sensible use of data in the context of instruction would allow teachers to "divide and differentiate" only if there were enough caring and intelligent bodies in the building to give each student the attention they required. And he knew that all this could be nurtured within and sustained by a culture that took the reality of students' lives into account: the food, housing, and economic insecurity, the physical violence that students observed if not experienced, the family instability that too many knew.[2]

When Sawyer left that evening, he had plans. He was going to blow up the one-teacher, one-classroom model of schooling. He would reconstitute the school, building crosscutting teams of teachers, led by accomplished educators who would *lead without leaving the classroom*. The teams would have control over curriculum, schedule, and grouping for their scholars, and the time in their day to collaborate. And he would establish and fund a culture team, integrated with the grade-level instructional teams, to support teachers' work with scholars.

The additional relational capacity would come from Vanderbilt residents who would work with scholars as they learned to teach in and through practice. While there would be lots of challenges, the crux of Sawyer's vision was clear: care for the teachers who will care for the scholars.

The spring semester of Sawyer's first year as principal was a whirlwind of planning for change. Sawyer's first move was to hire Dr. Claire Jasper, an experienced special educator and school leader, as chief of culture. Jasper was given a budget to hire the deans, counselors, social workers, community liaison officers, and special educators who were integral to the kind of trauma-informed and restorative culture they hoped to construct. This culture team knew the social, economic, and emotional circumstances of the kids' lives and would build a culture that valued where they came from while enabling them to move beyond those circumstances. They would become the "scholars" Sawyer imagined. Love and limits would go hand in hand.

The second move was to identify those teachers who had what Claire Jasper called "a heart for the work" and who had demonstrated the capacity to teach and lead, and to make them team leaders—not as coaches who did not work directly with kids, but in hybrid roles that tapped their abilities to teach, to coach, to analyze data and respond to it in practice, and to lead others in the collaborative processes that required. Those team leaders would be compensated for both their expertise and their extra effort. And then they were asked—collaborating with members of the culture team—to recruit and hire others with the same heart and willingness to learn what they didn't know about pedagogy and possibility for these scholars in this environment. Identifying educators of color to join the team was a priority.

The third step was to co-create the residency program that brought second-year Vanderbilt masters candidates into the school for the year, embedded full-time on instructional teams. Their presence (and modest pay) expanded relational capacity while keeping costs down, *and* supported the development of a cadre of caring, talented teachers who wanted to work with students who most needed them.

The fourth step was to find the money for all this. This was yet another exercise in response-ability, an exercise in letting go of some of the things that every school has. Small amounts of grant money helped. Also, by locating leadership, curricular and instructional planning, data analysis, and discipline within the crosscutting grade level and content teams, some other school-wide positions became unnecessary and funds could be redeployed.

Pedagogical Response-ability

In 2012, the Bailey scholars ranked dead last in the state of Tennessee in their literacy achievement and growth. It didn't take much pedagogical acumen to realize that treating reading and writing as one separate "subject" among the tested array (literacy, mathematics, science, and social studies) was not a winning strategy. Dr. Sawyer determined that, as a first step, English language arts and social studies would be combined in a placeholder called "Global Literacy" with teams of teachers (an English teacher, a social studies teacher, at least one resident specializing in either discipline, an exceptional educator, and a paraprofessional) coming together to construct a global literacy learning experience around the standards and texts prescribed by the state and district. The team had a double-block of time and the schedule flexibility to divide the total block into two, three, four, or even five subblocks focused on reading, writing, speaking, listening, and thinking, making use of fiction and nonfiction texts and long form and short form texts (including book, poetry, essay, etc.) that highlighted social studies content and modes of inquiry.

The teacher teams' autonomy was a double-edged sword, of course. There is real work involved in determining a curriculum that will interest students who have generally not been successful in school. Crafting what is culturally responsive and culturally sustaining—and also faithful to broader public expectations—is time-consuming and difficult. It is also rewarding and even joyful when students respond with ideas and energy.

Curricular decisions weren't all creative; that's neither possible nor desirable. Teachers made use of prescribed curricular materials to save time, to meet district expectations, and to participate in supported research. But that didn't mean that they accepted anything uncritically.

One prominent example included the implementation of the READ 180 curriculum, a grades 4–12 targeted reading intervention then being studied by a Vanderbilt University professor. The program consists of "high interest content" and "adaptive technologies" and promises "two years of growth" in one year. It offers "smart tools" to "save teachers time" and "data-driven teaching made easy," incorporating reading, writing, listening, speaking, and thinking in an integrated program. READ 180 could not constitute the whole of global literacy—there was virtually no history or social studies content—but it was intended to provide tools and formats to differentiate and personalize specific literacy skills. The Bailey teachers could see and appreciate all this. They could make use of the materials that guide and track their actions as teachers. However, they also recognized that the "high interest content" actually wasn't. That is, the books made available through the program were either naively romantic or *faux* scary for students who were worldly wise beyond their year—living, as many did, in the largest and most dangerous housing project in Nashville. Scholars didn't just resist the materials; they rejected them outright.

The teachers faced a dilemma that turned out not to be a dilemma at all: either enact the program "with fidelity" (using the given materials), or repurpose the program tools with texts that appropriately challenged the scholars intellectually and emotionally. They viewed the latter as more fitting—and more responsible, more in accord with the image of the teacher they wanted to be for their students—and immediately rounded up, with Dr. Sawyer's help, class sets of Young Adult books and also identified accessible online historical resources. The tools of READ 180 could be employed productively with more interesting and challenging texts for both skill development and meaningful comprehension.

Personal Response-ability

I spent nearly four years visiting Bailey Middle School regularly, usually spending one full day a week in the building. In the first year, not-yet-scholars would run down the hall (as middle school kids are wont to do), smash into me, bounce off, and run on, seemingly oblivious to the fact that they had just been part of a collision with another human being. They didn't see me and they didn't register "collision." In the second year, scholars were still running, but would often actually see me at the last minute, put out their hands to ward off a full-frontal collision, and dart around me with just a backward glance that said "oops." Still, I was a person, not an obstacle, and avoiding collision was somehow desirable. In the third year, there was less running; scholars were actually watching where they were going, aware of the people and events around them, and avoiding collision. When there was a collision, or even near-collision, they would look stricken and at least mutter "excuse me," or "sorry." Many even knew me by name and took advantage of the opportunity presented by (literally) running into me to stop and chat, share something about their lives or about their learning. By the fourth year, running in the hallways was rare, a sign that a scholar knew he was late and (responsibly) sought to get to class on time. Nobody ran into me.

At some point, I realized that this was data, data pointing to a developing response-ability in the Bailey scholars. The kind of responsibility the Bailey family (teachers, leaders, staff) targeted for the scholars (and the scholars came to target for themselves) was much richer than this, of course. Nonetheless, this anecdote captures something about student growth over time, growth in critical awareness, in developing interpretation and response, in the capacity for caring attention and rich relation, in realizing and taking responsibility, and in staying open to new people and new challenges.

Responsibility Beyond Accountability

Christian Sawyer and the Bailey educators faced a situation that was challenging, to say the least. They succeeded, not because they followed tried-and-true formulas, not because they were obedient to the directives of the district office or the state department of education, not because they demonstrated best professional practice, but because they took the time to pay attention to the actual needs of people in specific circumstances, they prioritized relational realities and collaborative possibilities, they considered multiple options for action, they weighed options in light of shared goals and values, they acted with confidence, and they reconsidered when the results didn't move them and their students closer to growth. In short, they prioritized response-ability, their own and their students, over accountability to external directives, research findings, and even "professional" habits. They did this in the overlapping domains of policy and protocol (edu-political response-ability), teaching and learning interactions (pedagogical response-ability), and individual growth in community (personal response-ability) sketched earlier.

This is not to say that directives, findings, and habits didn't inform and impact their individual decision-making or their collaborative action, only that responsibility requires agency rather than unquestioning obedience (whether to another, to an idea, to past practice). Sometimes old habits require reconstruction, often abstracted research findings are not easily translatable to concrete settings, and too often directives are fashioned by those removed from the action. When this is the case, there is no substitute for response-ability, for renegotiating the fitting response. When we reduce the rich possibilities described in the opening vignettes to *accountability*, that is to a burden imposed by external authorities or developed through unconscious socialization, the actual experience of responsibility is overlooked entirely. This prevailing sense of responsibility as accountability is simply not the only way responsibility can be understood. It is not especially fruitful—and may even be the source of misdirection—when we think about responsibility in the context of ethical educational practice.

In what follows, I try to loosen the hold that the notion of accountability has on our educational imaginary and replace it with a concept of responsibility that begins in educators' and students' capacity to respond to complex and challenging situations with fitting action, and *in responding*, to take responsibility for their individual and collective actions. To do this, I analyze the ways we use the terms "responsibility" and "accountability" in everyday settings and question whether these rhetorical uses reflect our actual purposes; I examine how philosophical understandings of responsibility have shifted over centuries to become less rooted in individual autonomy and free will and more representative of the relational interaction that make us moral persons; I sketch a view (a critical pragmatist view) of what educational judgment might be and how it might be practiced if response-ability is the starting point; and I link all of this to a particular site—Bailey STEM Magnet Middle School—where I watched this happen. The story I tell here through language analysis, the history of ethical theory, the construction of a critical pragmatist alternative view, and the lived experience of the leaders, teachers, students, and families at Bailey has no room for accountability as the justification of blame or punishment. In the end, I think you will see that accountability as a concept is not exactly wrong, just unnecessary—and unhelpful—with respect to educational practice worthy of the name.

In rejecting accountability as necessary to moral action in education, I am not denying the value of duty or obligation to one's self- and communal-understanding. Responsibility can be a yoke taken up by a person in community to give one's life meaning. It is accepted (perhaps not exactly freely but knowingly) because it is as Aristotle might have said, the right thing, at the right time, for the right reasons. It *fits* the situation. It is who I am and what I do, not simply as an individual, but as a person in interaction and community with others. That I am willing to be held accountable, that is, perhaps even to be blamed and punished for my actions, emerges from my capacity to recognize the need for response (my action—or inaction—in a situation only partly of my own making), *and* acting responsively to actual persons, nonhuman beings, and even the natural environment. But that is a burden I take on in becoming myself, not a burden that another imposes. Accountability as it is used in educational and political discourse today does not necessarily imply or even allow for real responsibility.

The external answerability I acknowledge connects responsibility to what philosophers call normative ethics, that is, the codified ethical norms and principles that capture how one *ought* to act. But normative ethics, useful though it is as an expression of what is generally expected in a community, is not the end of ethics (Dewey, 1891/1976: 241–2). It does not tell us what to do *now*; it cannot compel action. It can only tell us what has been done in similar settings in the past and prompt us to take that into account. Normative ethics is the titrated remainder of life in community without the actual lived tension of choosing this and not that in a particular situation. When education is the task at hand, it is not enough to work with the remainder. We—leaders, teachers, and students—have to go in search of the experience that makes value in living and learning.

I have been employing the idea of response-ability to make similar points about teaching, philosophizing, and program building for several decades (see, e.g., Stengel, 1999, 2001), but it is important to acknowledge that others have offered this phrasing, mostly in the context of feminist theorizing about ethics, culture, and education.[3] Nel Noddings (2003) employs "response-ability" in her classic, *Caring: A Relational*

View of Ethics and Education, referring to "a capacity neither essential nor innate, but learned and developed in actual life with other beings" (41). Rauna Kuokkanen (2007: 39), links response-ability to hospitality toward the other in her studies of Indigenous people's struggles with colonialism, describing it as "an ability to respond, to respond to the world beyond oneself, as well as a willingness to recognize its existence." Feminist philosopher Kelly Oliver (2018) offers an ethic of responsibility that starts with "the observation (emerging from phenomenological insight) that response is a capacity, not an automatic reaction." It is through an openness to address and engage with other people that the ability to respond adequately to the needs of other people increases.

In feminist New Materialist Karen Barad's agential realism (2007), "'responsibility' is not about right response, but rather a matter of inviting, welcoming, and enabling the response of the Other. That is, what is at issue is response-ability—the ability to respond" (2012: 81). Donna Haraway (2016) echoes Barad in claiming that epistemology (knowing) and ontology (being) come together here to instantiate "cultivating response-ability," an ethic that both requires and demonstrates "dynamic, moving relations of attunement." For Haraway, response-ability is the linchpin of living and dying well.

Each of these feminist philosophers offers not a principle-based ethic of rules to be followed, nor a virtue ethic of dispositions to be developed, nor a consequentialist view of means to achieve ends. It is a recognition that we are always responding to a world only partly of our own making and that the ability to respond richly and well is a collaborative capacity, not simply an individual attribute. This kind of approach to ethical action can be seen in all the waves of feminisms from Elizabeth Cady Stanton and Sojourner Truth through Jane Addams and Anna Julia Cooper through Carol Gilligan and Nel Noddings through bell hooks and Emily Townes to Haraway herself. Haraway goes further to incorporate

> emerging kinds of beings and ways of life of an always evolving home world. The Speakers for the Dead seek and release the energies of the past, present and future Chthulucene, with is myriad tentacles of opportunistic, dangerous and generative sympoeiesis. The Children of Compost would not cease the layered, curious practice of becoming-with others for a habitable, flourishing world. (2016, p. 163)

Still, a vision of "becoming-with others for a habitable, flourishing world" has always marked a feminist ethic of response-ability.[4]

Responsibility is the right educational anchor in a world in which we know everything and yet we know nothing. That we need an anchor, that we are drifting unmoored educationally in the twenty-first century, is part of the argument I make here. That responsibility—*originating* in and developed as a prospective capacity (response-ability) rather than retrospective accountability—is the right anchor is my central claim.

In fact, I would go further to insist that education and an ethic of response-ability are two sides of the same coin. This is what too many—though not most educators—have lost sight of in public discourse. Policymakers talk about education in terms that erase the embodied, interactional, cognitively challenging, and affectively charged experience involved. They create systems that measure and classify students, teachers, schools, and districts by test scores as if scores tell us what we—as educators or as citizens—need to know. They (and we, I'm afraid) talk about responsibility as if accountability is its only face, neglecting responsibility's origins in one's experience of oneself. With both education and responsibility, *experience* cannot be forgotten. I mean this literally not prescriptively. It is not just that we should not forget, but that we are not able to shed the experience that brought us to this place, however we veil it. Our lived reality will confront us again and again. The experience of responsibility that powers and makes sense of human living and the education that enriches it brings cognition, affection, and action together in a meaningful mix. That mix acknowledges past histories of association, marks the present moment in all its richness, and lends direction (for the immediate future) to a life well-lived.

Parallel Stories

Responsibility is the clarion call of schooling for *all* who play a role in it. Students, parents, teachers, leaders, and even policymakers generate responsibility for their efforts, often without awareness of the ways they are responding and even without consciously acknowledging the complex situations that prompt response rather than simple reaction. And although the notion of responsibility is rarely applied to the institution of schooling itself, it might well be. That is, how can a school be designed so that all persons in it are response-able, being and becoming both smart and good, working toward outcomes that are generative, just, and equitable?

Here I tell parallel stories—one philosophical, the other educational and experimental—with a common "moral": that every educational interaction is a call to and opportunity for responsibility for all involved. The philosophical story is a critical pragmatist framing of the concept of responsibility as, first of all, response-ability in the realm of education. This framing more closely matches educators' (and students) lived experience of educational effort and moral responsibility and is therefore a promising approach to expressing educational meaning-making. That lived experience, introduced at the outset, is the second story: an actual experiment of students, teachers, aides, administrators, and others as they recreated a particular school in which all struggled to hear the call and take advantage of the opportunity to be and become responsible—for their lives-in-common and their individual well-being.

Why Responsibility/Response-ability? Why Now?

If you are paying attention, you are aware of two realities challenging educators today, one immediate and one longer term. The immediate concern is the aftermath of the worldwide Covid-19 pandemic and its impact on both student achievement and student mental and emotional health. Learning loss is a primary concern and solutions offered are generally unimaginative, focusing narrowly on high-impact tutoring. Mental health has unfortunately been relegated to the background. In the United States, school districts have substantial financial support to target pandemic impacts, support that must be spent within the next year. What is the understanding of schooling as academic, socio-emotional, and ethical that is guiding those expenditures?

The longer-term concern is that school boards and state legislatures in the United States are sites of hand-to-hand rhetorical, political, and occasionally physical battle over "culture war" issues—Covid-19 mask-wearing, homosexual "grooming," critical race theory, transgender bathrooms—that are tangential to the education of our young. The sad reality is that schooling today has become—in the United States at least—a political tool rather than an educative one. Commitments to school improvement strategies—school choice, standardized testing, trauma-informed instruction, culturally responsive pedagogy, enhanced teacher pay—serve as cover for a "deformed politics" (Brown, 2017)[5] that is really about cultural control. Is schooling a public good or a perverse monopoly? Staffed by dedicated educators or by cynical union members? Who are intent on indoctrinating youngsters in left-wing ideology or sorting students into the worthy and the unworthy? In other words, most of the ink spilled and rhetoric uttered around education today actually sidestep education completely. But this need not be the case. It *cannot* be the case if we take our task as educators seriously. How can we get (back?) to a more educative public discourse and pedagogical practice, one that can guide expenditures and actions toward truly educative outcomes?

Perhaps one way is to emulate Horace Mann's expansive statement of purpose in his twelfth Annual Report to the Massachusetts Board of Education in 1848. Mann, the first secretary of education in the Commonwealth of Massachusetts (and the first nationwide), documented five purposes for public education: physical, intellectual, political, moral, and religious. He sought to remind his constituents that education was a big job and it was not merely focused on the individual. While some of the outcomes in Mann's framing could be measured or documented by the performance of an individual in their daily actions and interactions, others were clearly about how one came to be a person in the world through social and cultural relationships.

Today, we hear calls for students to exit K-12 systems "college and career ready." While this has some immediate appeal, there are many problems implicit in that formulation. One is the suggestion that college ready and career ready are not the same thing. Another is the assumption that only some will be college ready, while others will be ready for careers that occupy lower status and garner lower wages. The larger problem is that limiting educational goals to "college and career ready" focuses only on the economic value of the individual. This emphasis on *homo oeconomicus* neglects life dimensions related to the arts, civic action, family, friendship, caregiving, or any of the other domains that enrich communities.

Another contemporary formulation might be "caring, competent citizens" courtesy of educational thinkers like Linda Darling Hammond (2000) and Nel Noddings (1993). I find this articulation of purpose richer than "college and career ready" in large part because it points beyond corporate value toward citizenship competence of various kinds, but also to caring interaction. Still, this formulation offers an end in view for students but no obvious guidance for teachers and policymakers. It tells us where we are heading, but not how to get there.

These purposes, the first a product largely of politicians influenced by corporate executives, the second a product of theory-minded educational researchers, are relatively innocuous, and you might find something to like in these slogans no matter your ideological position. In fact, the National Council for Social Studies Standards (2013), known as "the three Cs," sought to marry these two. Unfortunately, as schools have become mired in culture wars, we too often find school rhetoric and policymaking decoupled from the lived experience of children and adults in schools.

Whatever you think about how we have found our way to a hyper-politicized state in public education, we can agree that the political machinations of the day have conspired to drain richness from the educational experience of many, if not most, children. There is no room for the expressions of humanity that make life worth living (e.g., aesthetic and religious experience). There is woefully little cultivation of the intrinsic joys of inquiry. In short, we fail to address whether the experience of teachers and students in schools is actually educative. We fail as well to acknowledge that all schooling is always ethical as well as political and that the search for and construction of what we have in common is a critical element in the very possibility of public (and publicly mandated) schooling.

It is not an accident that the term I offer to focus *and* expand our thinking is associated with both the history of ethics and the understanding of human persons as political animals. Education, politics, and ethics are intertwined in more ways than I have time to take up here, as Aristotle knew and John Dewey claimed explicitly. It makes sense to enter the field of education using language that points us in the direction of both the ethical and the political. This is not to suggest that there is not both an art and a science to the practice of teaching. However, both art and science can be narrowed to means rather than ends, constraining us from holding purpose central in any deliberation about what to do and how to do it. Responsibility is a robust enough term, rooted in (ethical and political) purpose, to tether educators to their own moral and professional motivations and to connect both parents and public to worthy goals for students individually and society collectively.

Always Political

Education, whether formally intended or informally experienced, is always political. For much of American educational history, the politics have been obscured by the dominance first of a controlling white Anglo-Saxon Protestant ideology and later by a turn to "professionalism" (Tyack & Hansot, 1981). However, since the 1960s, it has been impossible to hide the political motivations raising a ruckus in the schoolhouse. That onslaught has come from the political left as various groups rally for racial justice, equitable conditions and compensation for teachers, services for kids with disabilities, and LGBTQ rights. It has also come from the political right formed as efforts to undercut the very idea of common schools in favor of individual "choice" and narrowed claims of patriotism.

Can aspiring democracies respond to this conflict? This is complicated today by the rise in authoritarian strains in governments throughout the world, as Marine Le Pen in France, Donald Trump in the United States, and Jair Bolsonaro in Brazil resurface old grievances. A second complicating factor is the shape of our individual and collective economies: Will capitalism defeat the very possibility of democracy (moving us toward autocracies that preserve the wealth of the few in the name of freedom?) or will democracy bend capitalism to its parameters (prioritizing equality as a regulative ideal shaping the structure and play of markets of all kinds)? The colonial project around the world foregrounded wealth acquisition, followed in modern times by a relentless project of protecting the wealth so acquired from the grasping hands of governments. Politics is "deformed" as I and Wendy Brown (2017) have already noted. Nonetheless, as an educator, I continue to believe that we are presented with false dichotomies, that both resistance and constructive action are possible and required, and that a pragmatist ethic of responsibility points the way, not simply to reforming politics but to responding constructively to the admittedly precarious situations we currently inhabit.

That there is conflict about the purposes, processes, and products of schooling is acceptable and even positive if there is some shared means of making sense of the conflict and forging what pragmatist Mary Parker Follett (1995) called "creative integration." That is precisely what we don't have in a political environment in which thinking is frowned upon, feelings are hardened rather than flowing, and acts are set in stone rather than responsive to circumstances. Historians David Tyack and Elizabeth Hansot (1981: 23) point out that "[I]f people forget what animates institutions, [the institutions] atrophy." This is the present state of affairs in American schooling.

I propose responsibility, understood at its root as "response-ability," as a candidate for what animates schooling in America and in any nation that seeks democracy in practice not just in rhetoric. Responsibility so conceived is not an ideology that unites by force of agreement, but a way of acknowledging common humanity (i.e., this *is* how we think), establishing a means to communicate, ensuring that the competing values underlying positions are revealed rather than obscured, and recognizing the virtue and value of all those diverse others with whom I inhabit my world(s).

The present moment—political, theoretical, and concrete—requires a mode of thinking about education that is re-energized as it is redefined, that is accessible and invites broad participation. In the present moment we are immobilized when it comes to education; we need to be moved. We need to learn how, in George Saunders' (2007: 55) idiom, we can be open to possibility, and stay "so open it hurts." Only then can we ensure that what we are pursuing is worthy of the name education.

"Responsibility" is not a slogan we can put on a banner we all wave, but an acknowledgment that the only option in the world we have created—a world where we seek what is certain and instead encounter what is precarious, is to respond in community, to seek a better way to navigate that world together.

Chapter Outline

The structure of this book follows roughly the pattern of my argument. Chapter 2 takes up the language of responsibility as we have traditionally thought about and enacted it as accountability, and then moves to track changes in framing the concept of responsibility before and after Nietzsche. I consider, in particular, continental philosophers of the early and mid-twentieth century, American pragmatists in the first half of the twentieth century, and female British ethicists in the mid-twentieth century. Chapter 3 brings those insights to bear on the framing of a critical pragmatist ethic of responsibility as response-ability *for* educational policy, practice, and purpose. In both of these chapters—as in this Introduction, I move back and forth between an authorial voice that can be characterized as abstracted from experience (a voice that seems philosophical) and one that conveys the concreteness of practice (and seems narrative, even novelistic). Both are, I submit, philosophical in that each represents a way of accessing the truth, meaning, and meaningfulness of the lived experience of response-ability that we seek to understand.[6]

Chapter 4 explores response-ability as a design principle for policymakers and leaders (edu-political responsibility), as a pedagogical guide for teachers (pedagogical responsibility), and as a statement of purpose and desired achievement for students (personal responsibility), using concrete examples from the lived experience of Bailey Middle School. Here the voice is admittedly pedagogical, but informed by a critical pragmatist sensibility. The distinguishable abstracted and concrete voices in the early chapters find an integration in the lived experience of the Bailey crew.

In the final chapter, I think through what the critical pragmatist shift from accountability to response-ability gives and takes away, highlighting the synergistic and self-correcting qualities of this approach to the practice of education. The chapter also includes a postscript on the Bailey experiment.

CHAPTER 2

Responsibility Reconsidered

In this chapter, I continue to claim that blame, punishment, and accountability are not the most fruitful starting points for thinking about responsibility, despite a common tendency to do just that *and* despite the philosophical history that points to praise and blame as critical moral concerns. The central moral issue, the key to understanding responsibility, is not whether you deserve blame and punishment for something you have done in the past, but whether you have the capacity to respond well to the situation in which you find yourself in the present. This is response-ability; it is response-ability that makes responsibility possible.

Responsibility, that is, the willingness to say "I did this and accept the consequences" is not the same as accountability, that is, another's intention to make you "pay" for what you have done. The concept of accountability only makes sense as part of a moral framing that starts with blame and punishment *because it presumes that moral (or legal) codes preexist relation, encounter, and lived experience.* Already-given precepts for action (framed by cultural tradition or religious creed, for example) dictate the quality of one's behavior in advance. In such a framework, the only complication is whether one has acted freely and autonomously, that one has not been forced against one's will to transgress.

I say again that I am not jettisoning the idea of responsibility as the willingness to yoke oneself to social norms and to persist in honoring those norms. Nor am I denying that there are social and educational covenants that warrant the practice of accountability. I am, however, suggesting that accountability is a dangerous if sometimes useful concept. In educational settings, it is far too easy to implement systems of accountability (for students or schools) that actually impede rather than encourage responsive teaching and generative learning.

Imagine, then, an ethical conception of education that has responsibility, not accountability, as its anchor concept. Think first of responsibility as the ability of a competent agent to respond in a fitting way to ever-changing, ever-challenging, and multifaceted world(s). It is only by prioritizing the agency of persons that I can articulate a defensible view of education that revolves around responsibility.

To prioritize response-ability, we have to bracket what we take for granted about responsibility as a moral duty preexisting any social circumstance or interaction and describe more precisely the experience of response-ability. In this chapter, I do that work by, first, considering how we use the term in everyday speech, and then, rehearsing briefly the philosophical and ethical theories that have lent responsibility its dominant sense, as well as the more recent theorizing that challenges responsibility as accountability.

I am under no illusion that what I offer here will cause all of us to change how we employ the term "responsibility," nor should it. Language use simply cannot be dictated. What I can do is make a case that a reconstructed idea of responsibility can both reflect the best available thinking about ethical action and, at the same time, carry important weight and convey important meaning for educators and those who care about the education of the young.

"Responsibility" in Ordinary Use

We tend to think of ethics as a system of rules or virtues, and of responsibility as "living up to" whatever the rules demand or the virtues require. Most of us have heard some version of Aesop's Fable about the ants and the grasshopper. The ants work all summer, eschewing the fun the grasshopper espouses, to get ready for the winter, saving seeds, and storing whatever is needed to survive the harsh weather. They seem unswayed by the grasshopper's invitation to "come and have fun with me." In the end, of course, the ants have stores for the winter and the grasshopper is literally out in the cold. The moral of the story, implied as obvious, is that sacrificing joy to industry is an obviously moral choice and that anyone (human as well as ant or grasshopper) has the capacity to make such a prudential choice unmoved by other considerations of emotion and connection (or in the case of the grasshopper, genetic destiny).

It is important to prepare for the future, suggests Aesop. And so it is. But can a human life be all future-oriented prudence and no present-oriented enjoyment—and still be *human*? In many, perhaps most, situations, preparing for the future is praiseworthy, but Aesop is not right that the future always outweighs the present in thinking-into present action. Moreover, consider the possibility that socio-economic context constrains who has the luxury of thinking about the future, or about what kinds of choices are even possible. Aesop's moral is worth considering, but it is just one consideration among many in shaping action in the here and now. Responsibility lay not simply in following Aesop's lesson, but in the determination of whether *that* lesson fits *this* situation.

Responsible/Responsibility

The terms "responsible" and "responsibility" crop up in our conversation often, especially when values and beliefs are implicated. Some uses seem personal and practical. One might say, for example, "Because I didn't have adequate health insurance, I am responsible for paying the bill for my surgery." Some uses are institutional, obviously linked to designated social roles. For example, "As an employer, it is my responsibility to ensure that my employees are paid a fair and living wage." Some uses are cultural. "As a white woman in a racist world, it is my responsibility to allow room for people of color to speak their truth." When the intention is explicitly educational, the use of responsibility talk is pedagogical. "As a teacher, students' mastery of the standards is my responsibility."

In each case, there is a political dimension that is more or less obvious. Why and how are norms and values with regard to healthcare, employment, race realities, and educational goals set? Who is responsible (who is to praise or blame?) for creating the conditions under which these statements make sense?

It is impossible to determine whether each individual's claim of responsibility is prospective and in the present or retrospective and linked to maintaining the status quo until we finish the sentence and understand the political conditions that frame the claim. Is the speaker claiming response-ability or is she rehearsing responsibility pre-formed and externally given by those with the power to control the narrative?

Change the "I" in each example to "you" and the determination is easier. There are, I suggest, three "tells" that mark the praise/blame view of responsibility as accountability. These may occur in tandem or separately.

1. The first is the second-person statement. *You* are responsible (a) for specific action, for having done it, (b) for the consequences of it, and (c) for another's well-being. When one assigns responsibility to another, it is almost always a setup for accountability.
2. The second is the first-person statement but without the power to respond. I am responsible but my only option is to enact/react, without interpretation and response.

3 The third is the absence of relationality. If there is no identifiable other toward whom my response takes shape, there is no opportunity for responsiveness.

It is not always the case that another's second-person statement rules out my claim of personal, political, or pedagogical response-ability. Nonetheless, these tasks may also constitute a burden externally imposed and in conflict with deeply held values. As one who believes that health care is a universal right, that just wages lend reality to the possibility of democracy, that racism's end depends on all of us, and that state standards both help and hinder the growth and well-being of students, I take on this responsibility willingly. But another who challenges these values will reject this assignment of responsibility.

Consider another set of responsibility claims: "Who is responsible" for the mess in the room, for letting the dog out unleashed, for the shooting in the street, for the rioting after police brutality, for the child who cannot read? Note the progression from an individual who fails to do something to the systems that make it difficult, if not impossible for something to happen. What do I ask in each case?

In each case, the use of "responsibility" points to a preset ordering of social tasks that have not been fulfilled. There are tasks that (apparently) need to be done, someone (or some collective) has to step up and do them, and if the tasks are not taken up by the appropriate party, there could be consequences negative enough to justify "punishment" in the form of critique or sanctions. In the context of family, it is easy to agree that "we" want to and do clean up our messes and care for our dogs, at least usually. But as we make the circle of "we" bigger, and more impersonal, it is difficult to accept and assign responsibility for problems that become increasingly complex.

The problem, of course, is the preset ordering that assigns blame on the basis of institutionalized assumptions that may be, if not wrong, at least limited. On what basis are claims of blame legitimate? Who decides? Whose interests are served when negative consequences are imposed or even threatened? And how is the rhetoric of responsibility employed to shift a burden or to deflect (or focus) blame, especially with respect to race, class, nationality, or gender? How can responsibility be weaponized against those who lack power or who seek power?

When viewed this way, responsibility is reduced to accountability, absent any consideration of capacity for response. It constitutes a burden, not of our own choosing, unresponsive to the persons we encounter, disconnected from the person we are or are becoming. In general, accountability is not something one seeks, *unless* one sees it as a moment on an identifiable journey toward freedom, adulthood, material reward, and so on. Those who assign responsibility to others are not inviting response-ability, but using their power and privilege to shift the burden of action and consequence.

One can be held accountable by "authorities" through various forms of punishment. (It is worth noting that we don't use the expression "held accountable" when we are *praising* one's action.) If you are responsible, then you can be punished. But a basic question confronts us: (Why) Do we need justification for punishment? It is not clear that we do, either as part of an ethical system or as part of any educational effort (Kohn, 1993). Put simply, the response and responsiveness at the etymological and phenomenological heart of the concept of responsibility are lost in the everyday use of the term. Instead, *some* wield "responsibility" to justify holding *others* accountable.[1]

There are alternatives to this juridical and punitive ethical vision, and we can find them in various literatures from the New Testament to the thinking of Buddhist nun Pema Chodron and the (perhaps pop) psychology of Brenè Brown. Often these alternatives intensify the ideas of response and responsiveness in remarkable ways that tie one's very being to responsibility. In an essay entitled "Ethics" in his recent collection *Black Paper*, Teju Cole (2022) feels

> compelled to consider what it might mean to abandon the conventions of "raising awareness," of what it might mean to commit to the more dangerous work of bearing witness. The one who merely raises awareness can still pretend to neutrality, while the one who bears witness has already taken sides, has already committed to being unprofessional. (193)

I note this only to establish that the version of response-ability that I take up here is not in any way an abdication of the need for an energy that serves the purpose of accountability in our social interaction, that is, to call out for myself and the other what is needed and what might be demanded in a given situation. Here I seek only to reveal the roots of that responsibility in ways that make it more vibrant and, ironically, more freely accepted.

Admittedly, responsibility carries with it a sense of obligation imposed (in its accountability guise) or of substantive weight that one takes up or puts down as one is able (in its response-ability form). Adulthood is generally measured by a willingness to take on the weight of a committed relationship, a "regular" job, the rearing of children, and the purchase of a home. For youngsters and adolescents, responsibility is found in approximations of these adult tasks.

This is very often unproblematic and even positive; in truth, it is the better part of children's socialization. Parents, teachers, and coaches hold out opportunities for practicing response-ability and taking responsibility that youngsters can step into, try on, and make their own. But responsibility, especially when it is cloaked as "moral" responsibility, can become a cudgel wielded to control others by obscuring their own best interests. Responsibility becomes shorthand for expectations imposed without the invitation for critique and reconstruction.

Admittedly, parents are generally trying to keep their children safe while expanding their horizons. Teachers want to push children to master the tried-and-true while freeing them to think the new. There is simply not enough time to rethink every parenting or pedagogical habit. But there is a danger. If there is no possibility to think again, both parenting and teaching are reduced to teachers and parents doing to children what was done to them, rather than interpreting the reality of children's lives and responding to what they see. Habituation dominates and punishment becomes a feature of a disciplinary system that is only too familiar to us. This is not even useful in prisons, but it is particularly counterproductive when the task at hand is education. The practice of useful (and time-tested) habits is always subject in principle to the meta-habit of rethinking and reconstructing what we take for granted.

Educators are required *as educators* to be open to rethinking and reconstructing habits, even when that rethinking upsets the applecart of their professional practice. To be closed to rethinking is to practice indoctrination rather than education.

Tracing Responsibility's Ethical Trajectory

Responsibility is not a new term in the lexicon of ethical (and political) thinking. We can trace it at least back to the Athenian Aristotle who linked the concept to undetermined choices and freedom. But as I will show here, the representation of responsibility as a moral/ethical concept has shifted dramatically since Nietzsche, and has been developed—in different, but complementary, directions—by continental, Anglo, and American philosophers over the past century. My purpose in this section is not to take up the impossible task of representing "responsibility" across its history but to provide some signposts convincing enough to confirm for you the shift in meaning and ethical possibility to which I point. In other words, I invite you to shed your habitual reliance on responsibility as accountability and take up the habit of thinking about responsibility (response-ability) as a capacity to be developed in relation.

After Aristotle

For Aristotle, one is responsible for one's acts when—and because—one can exercise one's will, freely and rationally. Because Aristotle offers this formulation framed by the question of when praise or blame is appropriate, there is a tendency to reduce moral responsibility to accountability.

Consider what Aristotle (1985) actually says about all this (from Book III of the *Nichomachean Ethics*). "Praise and blame require voluntary actions" (1110a 29). Then he distinguishes what is voluntary from what is involuntary: "What comes about by force or because of ignorance seems to be involuntary" (1110a 1). That which is "up to us," the "actions we can do," demand our deliberation (1112a 31). Deliberation focuses on means rather than ends ("We deliberate about things that promote an end, not about the end" (1113a 1–2)) and possibility rather than impossibility ("If we encounter an impossible step . . . we desist; but if the action appears possible, we undertake it" (1112b 25). Deliberation means that " . . . a human being would seem to originate action" (1112b 33–4). Action indicates the end of deliberation ("For each of us stops inquiring how to act as soon as he traces the origin to himself" (1113a 3–6)). If one is the originator of action, one can be praised or blamed.

While the presenting question is linked to praise and blame, Aristotle's actual interest is in the realm of human power or capacity. That capacity is linked to the space of the voluntary and the possibility of deliberation. The agent is both willful and cognizant, using reason to identify both the particulars of the situation and the good in nature. Still, there must be some kind of indeterminacy that provokes deliberation and the possibility of choice, and that deliberation resolves itself when we trace the action to one's own power.

Aristotle is concerned with what is "within our power" or "up to us." That makes obvious sense given his setup. If an event is not "up to us," then it is hard to impose external consequences for action. But if I both willed an action and powered or caused it, then I can be held accountable.

I highlight two features of Aristotle's position. The first is that Aristotle carves out separable spaces naming that which is voluntary and that which is not. The second is that Aristotle does actually point to responsibility as a phenomenon independent of its roots in the blame/praise problematic. He is not just describing the sphere of human agency as responsibility, but establishing it (Raffoul, 2010: 40).

Kant's project is not the same as Aristotle's, despite a common interest in the power and capacity of the person and a reliance on the agency as situated in that which is voluntary —and despite the way both positions ultimately reinforce a juridical praise/blame interpretation of responsibility. Where Aristotle turns outward to lived experience, Kant turns inward to transcendental intuition. Where Aristotle relies on the conception of a (privileged) person as a participant in a *polis*, Kant takes seriously the enlightenment subject understood as an atomistic and autonomous individual, who is worthy of respect and value because of that autonomy. While the practical import of Kant's position is that those who fail to obey the dictates of imperatives are subject to blame and punishment, his philosophical interest has much more to do with justifying the empowerment of the enlightenment individual.

Kant looks for and finds justification for a person's value in the "transcendental freedom" that distinguishes persons from things. Transcendental freedom, determining who is capable of absolutely and spontaneously beginning a new series of causes, is what grounds the possibility of "imputability." A person is a subject whose actions can be imputed to them. If one has the capacity and freedom to originate action, then that action can be associated with a person in a causal way. This opens the space of autonomy (self-responsibility) as well as responsibility as accountability.

In what is likely Kant's most accessible essay, "What Is Enlightenment?" (1784), he makes clear his concern with the individual's capacity for independent action. In well-known prose, Kant states his case:

> Enlightenment is man's emergence from his self-imposed nonage. Nonage is the inability to use one's own understanding without another's guidance. This nonage is self-imposed if its cause lies not in lack of understanding but in indecision and lack of courage to use one's own mind without another's guidance.

The full, transcendental freedom that Kant posits is freedom of thought (Raffoul: 58–79). But that freedom is not just possibility; it is one's responsibility as a human and it takes courage to employ this capacity fully.

The freedom that Kant prioritizes is not of this world. Kant (1784) acknowledges the paradox of his position that thought must be unfettered while action is reasonably subject to social constraints:

> Thus we observe here as elsewhere in human affairs, in which almost everything is paradoxical, a surprising and unexpected course of events: a large degree of civic freedom appears to be of advantage to the intellectual freedom of the people, yet at the same time it establishes insurmountable barriers. *A lesser degree of civic freedom, however, creates room to let that free spirit expand to the limits of its capacity.* . . . And this free thought gradually reacts back on the modes of thought of the people, and men become more and more capable of acting in freedom [emphasis added].

One is responsible to think freely in order to encourage sociopolitical conditions that can and will support the continued enlightenment of and respect for persons. "Dogmas and formulas" have to be challenged in one's public persona as a scholar while acting privately in concert with the demands of those formulas. The mode of moral deliberation (i.e., deliberation with respect to action) is discover-obey. One determines the guiding practices and principles and obeys them.

The dogmas and formulas that Kant acknowledges are mutable social constructs, subject to reconstruction when persons begin to challenge them with courage. But the philosophical concepts on which Kant depends—agency, causality, free will, intentionality, and subjectivity—are also social constructs. They are inherited fictions, useful but potentially dangerous.

My point in describing the ethical theories of Aristotle and Kant is not to suggest that taken-for-granted conceptions of responsibility as accountability mirror these philosophers' views—which are far more sophisticated than our everyday intuitions, but only to note that nothing in their views of responsibility challenges the ideas of individual accountability that dominate everyday speech. That changes with Nietzsche.

After Nietzsche

It is no secret that the story of modern thought since Nietzsche moves us away from the accountability of a free autonomous subject. How does Nietzsche get us there? He proceeds from the understanding that language doesn't just express or describe the world; it constructs world(s) and our knowledge of them (Nietzsche, 1996: sec. 11). Those worlds, indeed all human interaction, are power-laden and our views of those worlds are shaped by our own interests and blind spots (Raffoul, 2010: 86–8; Nietzsche, 1974). Human experience is at once affective, cognitive, and behavioral; there is no separating out what is "rational" (Raffoul, 2010: 82; Nietzsche, 1979). Any perception of "necessity" is a function of habit (Raffoul, 2010: 89). There is no easy divide between what is natural (or God-given) and what is human constructed. This requires acceptance of ethics and morality not as *a priori* directives but as social practice situated in cultural and political contexts (and institutions). And that in turn, opens the door to a careful reconsideration of the concepts of ethical action. Nietzsche's particular target is the very idea of accountability as he says directly in *Human, All Too Human:* " . . . the history of moral sensations is the history of an error, the error of accountability, which rests on the error of freedom of will" (Nietzsche, quoted in Raffoul, 2010: 80).

Thus morality cannot precede living. Nietzsche asks directly: "What are our evaluations and moral tables worth? What is the outcome of their rule? For whom? In relation to what?— Answer: for life" (Nietzsche, 1901/1967; sec. 254).

His method rejects what is "ideal," and shifts to the phenomenological: that is, "disregard intellectual clutter, pay attention to things and let them reveal themselves to you" (Bakewell, 2016: 3). The resulting shift moves from juridical to relational, from responsibility as socially enforceable burden to an (inter)personal answerability and responsiveness. It is a return to the "human, all too human" origin of ethics and values. The autonomous subject is not acknowledged in order to be accused and undermined. Instead, Nietzsche seeks to uncover responsibility's moment of origin, arising again and again, in human interaction. Where Aristotle begins with the problem of who can be praised and blamed, Nietzsche looks for relations of power that stipulate possibilities of praise and blame. Where Kant posits the transcendental subject as the sine qua non of morality, Nietzsche looks to answerability as the moment of encounter where morality comes to be (possible).

Interestingly, this shift makes responsibility *more* not less central to ethics and morality. We see that in the continental response to Nietzsche, and in the American pragmatist re-interpretation of the possibilities that responsibility offers.

The Continental Response

In *The Origins of Responsibility*, François Raffoul (2010) documents what he characterizes as the post-metaphysical sense of responsibility developed subsequent to the critical phenomenological method Nietzsche employed. In Raffoul's framing, responsibility constitutes the cornerstone of the ethics of a set of continental philosophers including Sartre, Levinas, Derrida, and others—and each informs the sense of responsibility that I commend to you here. It is a theory of moral action freed from its association with a metaphysics of will and subjectivity, freed from origins in any predetermined codes to which one can be held accountable.

Take Sartre's (and deBeauvoir's) existentialist view (Sartre, 1992; deBeauvoir, 1949; deBeauvoir, 1953). If truth itself is relational, then human existence precedes its essence. We who are human are irrevocably tasked with determining meaning, meaningfulness, and value. It is an absolute responsibility that we cannot escape. The burden of our necessary human freedom cannot be sidestepped or evaded; we are accountable to ourselves and not to some external ethic. The ethical is not a set of norms but a characteristic of existence. We are responsible for our very existence.

Simone de Beauvoir expresses this in her essay "The Ethics of Ambiguity" (1947), beginning with an epigram from Montaigne: "Life in itself is neither good nor evil. It is the place of good and evil, according to what you make it." She bemoans the tendency to eliminate the ethical ambiguity that cannot be escaped by privileging inwardness *or* externality, sensibility *or* transcendence, eternal life *or* the present moment. She rejects "reasonable metaphysics" and "consoling ethics," instead stating simply: "It is in the knowledge of the genuine conditions of our life that we must draw our strength to live and our reason for acting." Human decisions matter, not with respect to heaven and hell, but with respect to meaning in this moment.

Informed by the existentialist temper, but not by Sartre's individualistic framing of that temper, Levinas (1985) breaks with Kantian universalism (and complicates agency) by situating ethics in the encounter with the singular Other, and by claiming for ethics the place of "first philosophy." Being (selfhood as we might refer to it colloquially) takes shape when and only when one is responsive to the Other as mortal, that is, ultimately vulnerable. In other words, for Levinas, responsibility, the *necessary* response to the face of the Other, precedes consciousness and intentionality, indeed precedes knowing and understanding.

This has extraordinary implications when education is on the table. What does it mean to designate a decision as "ethical" (versus "prudential," for example) and what difference in thought and action does that designation demand? Once the ethical domain is opened up beyond a rational calculus of goods, rights and/or rules, are there any decisions or actions that don't have ethical implications? If social justice as *merely* political or ideological is walled off from the ethical as obligatory, is there any way to leap over that wall, to get from ethical response to social justice?

The Levinasian answer to both questions is an emphatic "Yes," but that doesn't provide us with any definitive mapping of the terrain. The challenge is finding the place where responsibility is called out and enacted. It is not a particular static territory but a gap between is and what could be, between call and inspired response, not a place in space but a moment in interaction. It is, as Clarence Joldersma describes it, the "call that disturbs the thought and felt present in the present without being present, coming in from the outside, from who knows exactly where—before we are ready to domesticate it . . . " (Joldersma, 2014: 15). It is "the gap between hope and action across which the animation of inspiration jumps creat[ing] room for an ethical relation" (20). Not all actions and decisions have ethical import but we cannot tell in advance which are which. The "gap" invites the ethical. Hopeful response marks its presence, "reorient[ing] the self-centered preoccupation of striving to live" (9). The ethical is the result of the breakthrough of relationality, especially with respect to the disenfranchised, those who have been rendered less than human by the intended and unintended corollaries of institutional arrangements. To find the ethical is to locate the moments where responsibility and hope are both in play.

It is from Derrida that we are called to understand deconstruction as responsiveness, a responsiveness that follows from the demand for response to a particular aporia—a perplexity or unavoidable doubt—that can be understood in its completion as "taking responsibility." This taking responsibility implies a sense that something more can be thought or done (despite the reputation deconstruction has acquired as wholly destructive). The grounds of morality are (regularly) renegotiated.[2]

These continental thinkers follow Nietzsche in rethinking ethical responsibility as something prior to and infinitely more than accountability. The continental articulations of ethics as first philosophy and response to another as what constitutes us as humans both enable and require that responsibility be central to morality *and that morality be understood as created by the act of response*. This constitutive response-ability is prior to any construction or imposition of accountability, skewering the notion of the preexisting and autonomous subject and prioritizing human encounters one with another.

However, it is not clear, to me at least, how far deconstruction can advance an affirmative program of action despite Derrida's insistence that it be employed as a way to open up possibilities. As American cultural critic Louis Menand (2014) points out:

> Deconstruction is a *via negativa*. It's good for getting down to . . . the mechanical level of language. But it can't bring anything substantive back, because anything substantive is subject to the rigors of deconstruction all over again.

Menand's comment helps to explain why the stance I claim here is informed by the continental tradition without being embedded in or restricted by it. Instead, you will see, I offer a (critical) pragmatist framing, one that is more obviously congenial to deliberation-into-action.

The American Interpretation

While philosophers on the European continent were rejecting views of responsibility rooted in a metaphysical view of subjectivity and free will, a cadre of philosophers and social reformers in North America were forging their own not-quite-metaphysical view of human (inter)action and its moral quality.

I offer a lengthy passage from John Dewey's *Human Nature and Conduct* in which he captures both what responsibility—understood socially and prospectively—can be and how his view of responsibility transforms or, in his terminology, reconstructs the sense of traditional claims of accountability.

> We are held accountable by others for the consequences of our acts. . . . We are disapproved, and disapproval is not an inner state of mind but a most definite act. Others say to us by their deeds we do not care a fig whether you did this deliberately or not. We intend that you *shall* deliberate before you do it again, and that if possible your deliberation shall prevent a repetition of this act we object to. The reference in blame and every unfavorable judgment is prospective, not retrospective. Theories about responsibility may become confused, but in practice no one is stupid enough to try to change the past. Approbation and disapprobation are ways of influencing the formation of habits and aims; that is, of influencing future acts. The individual is *held* accountable for what he *has* done in order that he may be responsive in what he is *going* to do. Gradually persons learn by dramatic imitation to hold themselves accountable, and liability becomes a voluntary deliberate acknowledgment that deeds are our own, that their consequences come from us. (Dewey, 1922/1979: 217)

Note that in this characteristically pragmatist framing, there is a social behaviorism at work. As Dewey would have it, we are—as youngsters or persons new to any activity—held liable or accountable by others with the (social or professional) authority to do so not for purposes of punishment but for purposes of future deliberation-into-action. Remember, "the reference in blame is prospective. . . . " Dewey does not reduce responsibility to accountability. The formation of a sense or habit of responsibility, achieved through the experience of being held accountable by others, is only the socialization part of the morality story; intelligent reconstruction of habits is the generative part.

Morality emerges when one's habits (akin to what Aristotle taught us to call virtues and values) come into conflict with the expectations of others (based on their virtues and values)—or sometimes even into internal conflict. It is this conflict, not unlike Derrida's *aporia*, that occasions moral deliberation. If there were no conflict, there would be no morality. The point of our reflection, our moral deliberation, is to review and possibly reconstruct already acquired habits through new or alternate responses in interaction. Those reconstructed habits become the basis for our own future action and our socialization of others.

The organization of *Human Nature and Conduct* reflects Dewey's stance and argument. In the first section, "the place of habit in conduct," Dewey considers the formation of habit and then describes how habits are enacted with respect to custom, character, and will. In that section, Dewey channels Aristotle's understanding of moral formation. In the second section, "the place of impulse in conduct," Dewey lays out how habits can be disrupted when challenged by conflict that evokes emotion and differing desires. Dewey's theory of emotion figures prominently (1894, 1895, 1922/1979).

In the third and final section, "the place of intelligence in conduct," Dewey describes the centrality of what he calls "the method of intelligence" in addressing instances of value and habit conflict. It is here that he makes a place for Kantian principles and consequentialist calculus in deliberating the fitting response and the taking of responsibility in the light of changing aims and conceptions of the good, but also with reference to past, present, and future. Of course, says Dewey, principles and consequences matter in moral deliberation, just as seemingly shared aims and dominant conceptions of the good matter. However, danger lurks when principles and aims reify, when consequences and conceptions of the good dominate without question. The danger as Dewey sees it, is that when the elements of morality are fixed, they "take men away from experience" (1922/1979: 164). For a pragmatist, that's a problem.

This circuit of habit and reflection is the rhythm of moral action. We act, presumably morally, out of established habit until our habits fail us, perhaps because a situation is novel or because we are interacting with different others or because we have outgrown certain values or practices. At that point, what Mary Parker Follett (1995) calls the "law of the situation" demands a new pattern of response and responsiveness.

This is Dewey's "pragmatic experimentalism," an approach that emphasizes deliberation about viable choices and actions, a naturalistic approach to ethical inquiry and development, and an evaluation of the likely and actual consequences of moral decisions and actions. The good and bad, right and wrong, virtue and vice, and prudence and imprudence all come into play (Dewey, 1932/1983). But Dewey's pragmatist view can be strengthened further by the practice of personal responsiveness and loving attention that Iris Murdoch identifies as the mark of the moral agent.

The Women Are Up to Something

(Lipscomb, 2022). While the continental philosophers cited here sought to deconstruct the autonomous individual actor accountable for his own freely chosen actions as well as the consequences of those actions, and the pragmatists found a way to reconstruct that actor as socially enacting thought, emotion, and habit, a cohort of women philosophers in Britain in the Second World War were challenging orthodoxy from a different direction. They were reacting not to the space cleared by Nietzsche but by the constrained understanding of ethics and morality in the Anglo philosophical domain. British ethics in the lead-up to the war had adopted a positivist flavor, denying that moral claims had any truth value but were simply expressions of approval or disapproval. This was a bridge too far for Cambridge-trained philosophers Mary Bosanquet Midgeley, Phillipa Scrutton Foot, Iris Murdoch, and Elizabeth

Anscombe. In their shared view, anti-realist ethical theorists weren't paying attention to moral and obviously immoral lives. Further, in their estimation, this approach viewed reason too narrowly.

All four women had a significant impact on the progression of ethical thought emerging from Britain during and after the Second World War. But one is particularly important for my project here. That is Iris Murdoch whose musings on attention and responsiveness as critical elements in moral action and in moral deliberation provide an important point of emphasis (if not exactly a corrective) to my framing below of an ethic of responsibility.

Murdoch, like Dewey, was asking what we *can* do in the face of moral conflict, and her primary prescription was not a recommendation for specific action but a practice: paying careful attention. Avoiding the existentialists' "tough sounding admonitions to pull yourself together and choose" that were "false to her experience of change and growth," became a priority (Lipscomb, 2022: 129). Murdoch found a vocabulary in Simone Weil's emphasis on "loving attention" and turned largely to novels and essays outside of philosophy per se to make her philosophical points. As Murdoch acknowledges in perhaps her best-known philosophical work *The Sovereignty of Good*, "I have used the word 'attention', which I borrow from Simone Weil, to express the idea of a just and loving gaze directed upon an individual reality. I believe this to be the characteristic and proper mark of the active moral agent" (Murdoch, 1970: 33).

In the first essay of *The Sovereignty of Good*, Murdoch offers a well-known example, that of a Mother-in-Law (M) who holds a less than generous view of her Daughter-in-Law (D), but who nonetheless "behaves beautifully to [D] throughout" (17). M might have settled into a rigid, unchanging view of D. But M is "intelligent and well-intentioned person, capable of self-criticism, capable of giving careful and just *attention* to an object which confronts her." Gradually M's perception of D changes because of that attention. She comes to view her daughter-in-law more generously as she is in the moment but also in a way that allows D to develop and grow.

Here is how Murdoch analyzes why M's activity is hard to characterize—not because it is hazy but precisely because it is moral.

> What M is *ex hypothesi* attempting to do is not just to see D accurately but to see her justly or lovingly. Notice the rather different image of freedom which this at once suggests. Freedom is not the sudden jumping of the isolated will in and out of an impersonal logical complex, it is a function of the progressive attempt to see a particular object clearly. M's activity is essentially something progressive, something infinitely perfectible. So far from claiming for it a sort of infallibility, this new picture has built in the notion of a necessary fallibility. M is engaged in an endless task. (22-23)

Because M can "look again," a vector of growth is possible. "Goodness is connected with knowledge . . . a patient and just discernment and exploration of what confronts one, which is the result not simply of opening one's eyes but of a certain perfectly familiar kind of moral discipline" (Lipscomb, 2022: 248).

Through sustained attention, M comes to see more and better, and in the process, relationships are strengthened, even healed. As Lawrence Blum emphasizes, for Murdoch attention involves activity on our part, directing the "just and loving gaze upon an individual reality" (Blum, 2022). And our capacity to act well when challenged "depends partly, perhaps largely upon the quality of our habitual objects of attention" (Lipscomb, 2022: 248).

Murdoch's corrective, that is, her insistence on careful attention as the mark of the ethical actor, is especially important to my effort to capture an ethic of responsibility for education (see Stengel & Casey, 2013), and particularly for education that takes the power and prospects of *all* youngsters seriously. As Murdoch knows and notes, the primary barrier to our seeing clearly and fully is not laziness or lack of will, but the stories we tell—as participants in communities, cultures, institutions—to make sense of our world. Those stories are always selective, always both helpful and limiting, and always laden with power and privilege (or their lack). Learning to see *through* the stories one lives by—*through* both in the sense of deconstructing dominant narratives and in the sense of acknowledging that one cannot think at all "without a bannister" (Arendt, 2021) is critical.

Insights Generative for Education

Since Nietzsche, then, at least three strands of theorizing have pushed us to look beyond moral accountability to response-ability by recognizing relation as the originary impulse for ethics, by complicating our experience and understanding of both reason and freedom, and by redirecting our attention. Continental deconstructionists share a natural attitude, a phenomenological temper, and an "inhabited philosophy" (Bakewell, 2016: 31) with the British women and the American pragmatists. All acknowledge that we are thrown into a world only partly of our own making, that the best we can do is respond richly and fittingly to what we encounter. They share a focus on living well and doing so by attending to life rather than to faith *or* reason. Each shared, more or less, Sartre's view that persons have to "decide what kind of world they wanted, and make it happen" (quoted in Bakewell, 11), but never alone. What they offer to us can be brought together in a critical pragmatist ethic of educational responsibility not because they capture the same ethic, but because they reveal *practices* that can be cultivated and enacted at once.

There is a radical edge to all of this, an edge that is "surprisingly revolutionary," one that encourages, even demands, a critical response to what is taken-for-granted. Whether we are trading in deconstruction, reconstruction, or loving attention, a phenomenological approach, richly descriptive, can "give us back the world we live in." "There are no easy rules for dealing with a world that both delights and confounds us, but describing lived experience as it presents itself provides a way forward" (Bakewell, 2016: 44).

If we enact response-ability *before* accountability in the conduct of education, that is, if response-ability is the design principle for leaders, the pedagogical guide for teachers, and the goal for students, that work will yield a mature version of responsibility for all involved, and will mark the enterprise as educational. On the other hand, if we limit educational efforts to the assignment and acceptance of responsibilities as duty or obligation in the course of socialization, neither educators nor students will arrive at the kind of responsibility that is made and taken on willingly. James Baldwin understood the radical nature of seeking response-ability as I describe it here in a quote that seems especially poignant now. In 1963, he noted:

> [T]he purpose of education finally, is to create in a person the ability to look at the world for himself, to make his own decisions, to say to himself this is black or this is white, to decide for himself whether there is a God in heaven or not. To ask questions of the universe, and then learn to live with those questions, is the way he achieves his own identity. *But no society is really anxious to have that kind of person around.* What societies really, ideally, want is a citizenry which will simply obey the rules of society. If a society succeeds in this, that society is about to perish. The obligation of anyone who thinks of himself as responsible is to examine society and try to change it and to fight it—no matter what the risk. This is the only hope society has. This is the only way societies change [emphasis added]. (Baldwin, 1963)

As an educator, I accept the paradox that Baldwin articulates. We face the challenge of perpetuating society, but acknowledge that as our students become conscious, they will necessarily begin to examine critically the society in and for which they are being educated. An ethic of responsibility, generated *through* the capacity to respond, and issuing *in* responsibility accepted because it reflects who one is in community, is the only mode of thinking that enables educators to face up to that paradox constructively.

CHAPTER 3

Heuristics for an Educational Ethic of Responsibility

I turn to pragmatism, critical rather than classical, as the ethical stance of greatest use in educational deliberation and action. Like education, pragmatism is a naturalistic, forward-looking, and developmental endeavor. Pragmatism's commitment to a rhythm of relationally tested habit and principle punctuated by thorough inquiry when the situation demands a novel (or at least renewed) response is the only defensible stance in the face of the indeterminacy that is built into education and the precarity that marks education in our time.

In a pragmatist frame, everything—habits, norms, values, even facts—can change, but not everything at once. From a critical perspective, there is much about our social worlds that invites if not demands change, and no change is unthinkable. It might seem that a critical pragmatist stance would expose us to unnecessary instability, but this is not so. The instability we fear is not a product of pragmatist deliberation but built into our social life in the form of conflicting values and practices. Critical pragmatism as a practice of deliberation enables us to face the uncertainty created by conflict and yields generally stable guidance in the lived context of durable and sustaining community.[1]

Normativity "exists," of course, as an ethical practice constructed in communal living over time. We are aware of norms and follow them even when we are not conscious of them—in everyday life (stopping at a red light), and in professional practice (evaluating students fairly, offering equal opportunity). Still, specific norms, while useful and durable, are always also revisable in the process of pragmatist inquiry. A deep understanding of the relational ground of human beings (á la Levinas, for example), a recognition of the role of attention (á la Murdoch) in enacting moral agency, and a willingness to consider the status quo critically are complementary to a pragmatist perspective and important features of what is outlined here.

Why Critical Pragmatism for Education?

My primary justification for adopting a critical pragmatist stance is this: *educators can actually educate by and through the practice of response-ability.* A pragmatist practice requires the conscious articulation of goals and purposes, encourages conservative (re)action as a matter of accepted habit initially, expands to thoughtful interpretation and response when habit fails or the identification of the problem is itself problematic, and makes room for diversity of culture and perspective as part of the interpretation process and in the rehearsing possibilities phase.[2]

Adopting a pragmatist stance will disturb some who might argue that pragmatism constitutes a naïve faith in "progress," a faith that human nature does not support.[3] What I most appreciate about pragmatism is that its focus is living, that the pragmatist asks, what *can* I do, despite the constraints evident in any circumstance, to make the present situation better? I ask not how do I make it right, nor even what is good or virtuous, but what constructive action can be taken here and now? As educators working with only somewhat malleable students, our challenge is not to "fix" things (in the sense of either repair or solidify) but to act in ways that enable greater flourishing. In that formulation, both means *and* ends are up for grabs, subject to reconstruction.

The view that I espouse here is open to and has a long history in the lived experience of women and others—the disabled, the queer, the Black and Brown, and the colonized—whose autonomy and even humanity have been questioned.[4] They have faced preexistent circumstances, social habits, that have evolved to reify certain social relations and to exclude them. Survival and sanity required that they question the status quo. These are the persons who most often suffered the blame and punishment of those in authority, a trend that continues today.

Radical attention and responsibility to the Other require acknowledging that what counts as normative exists within a power structure that privileges some. Looking at events in situ makes it impossible to ignore cultural and economic material conditions. Claiming that things could be other than they are, that social arrangements that would and could be just call forth a critique of what is, opens to and demands a critical perspective. When one starts with "what the known demands" (á la Dewey) or acts "as if we were called" (á la Levinas), we open immediately to that which is not taken for granted. Enriched by the continental understanding of response, by Murdoch's insistence on attention, and by the insights of contemporary critical theories (e.g., feminism, critical race theory, disability critical studies, and queer theory), a pragmatist ethic becomes a tool that fits the educational dynamic of conservation (social reproduction) *and* growth (reconstruction).[5]

In both lived experience and in theorizing, we see emergent a rich description of systems of responsibility as *response-ability*, identifiable in three moments: the fact of *response* as an unavoidable parameter of human action, the existential, ontological, and/or ethical imperative for *responsiveness* to the other, and the self-constructive act and result that *responsibility* enacts. What we take to be responsibility *simpliciter* is actually a social construction (and a *post hoc* abstraction) that might (always) be otherwise. A pragmatist perspective allows us to return to response, responsiveness, and response-ability in order to reconstruct "what one deserves." I draw out this philosophical view with a particular problem of practice in mind: what can be the proper purpose, pedagogy, and policy for education?

We are not turning our backs on the insights of moral philosophy, only placing those insights in the broader social contexts and lived experiences that educators cannot ignore. That is, educators are responding to individual habits and societal structures as conditions for growth and development. Quality of personal decision-making, relational interaction, group functioning, and institutional structures are all implicated. Educators seek—for and with their students—the capacity for being and becoming better in specific situations, for responding richly in situations only partly of our own making, and in the process, for recreating the conditions for future response and responsiveness. This is an ethic consonant with educational efforts and intentions.

The *aporia*, Derrida's gap that marks the demand for interpretation and response, *is* the site of response-ability. As Burke and Greteman (2022: 110–11) note in another context, "It is only by going through a set of contradictory injunctions, impossible choices, that we make a choice. If I know what I have to do, if I know in advance what has to be done, then there is no responsibility . . . I have to do this and not that and they do not go together."

In other words, the experience of responsibility is not the rules, nor the sensation of external burden, nor the fact of praise or blame, reward or punishment. Those elements mark a system of accountability imposed on—or sometimes independent of—the experience of responsibility. One doesn't *experience* responsibility until one responds to the *aporia*, the *absence* of already known directives and consequences, in which an informed and consequential choice must be made. The weight (felt only as a burden when imposed externally) comes from within, informed by and informing a developing sense of self; the consequences are naturally occurring, issuing from the action taken in situ. Creating this experience for young people is an integral part of the educational project. We don't have to hold a student or teacher responsible; they already are by virtue of their capacity to act. It is the task of the educator to encourage and coach the open and attentive attitude that seeks to uncover all that is at stake—and all that is and is not controllable—in any given situation. Gregory Pappas (2018) describes this as "getting all the cards on the table."

There are several additional criticisms of a pragmatist view of ethics and/or politics that might be considered here: that pragmatism is too reactive, that pragmatism is open to relativism, and that pragmatism is not going anywhere, that it's not getting us closer to ethical truth. As a philosophical issue, this is much larger than the scope of this book. It constitutes a question about the purpose of philosophy. In brief, my answer to these criticisms is itself a pragmatist one: ethical truth is not a matter of discovery once and for all, but the tentative and ever-testable result of an ongoing—and shared—process of inquiry in community, yielding what Dewey calls "warranted assertibility" and enough stability to face the precarity that is unavoidable. To characterize this as relativistic because it is responsive to actual lived experience fails to recognize the dialectic and relational interaction of persons with each other and the world. Whether or not specific actions are "too reactive" can only be determined by the reflection and response that pragmatist inquiry calls forth. In other words, a pragmatist perspective "fits" the kind of thinking that educators typically practice and, actually, cannot avoid by virtue of their commitment to both the growth of the student and the conservation of community.

A critical pragmatist ethic of educational responsibility is an invitation, not a prescription. We are invited to acknowledge both the value *and* the tentative status of that which is normative or habitual, to act out of habit in the rhythms of everyday living, but also to question and reconstruct those habits by reflection prompted by refocused attention, conflicting values, or failure to accomplish shared goals. What I offer here are two different but related heuristics for that reflective reconstruction. The first is a set of questions that highlight the concerns accompanying a response-ability stance, and that allow one to check one's own focus of attention, state of mind, and affective openness to what is other than taken for granted. The second serves as "training wheels" for those who aspire to develop a richer capacity for the reflective thought that reconstruction of habit requires.

Response-ability in Educational Action

Accepting the fact of response, responsiveness, and response-ability in any ethical or educational framing of human action presents us with a set of questions: (1) What does it mean to cultivate an actionable and constructively *critical perspective*? (2) How does an explicit habit or practice of *interpretation and response* extend and expand the possible actions open to any person in any situation? (3) What is gained and/or lost by *attending to relation* as intrinsic to responsibility? (4) How does one actively *make and take responsibility* (rather than have it imposed)? And (5) What are the (affective) costs and benefits attached to *embracing uncertainty and staying open* in the face of the recognition of limited control and constrained freedom? These questions constitute a heuristic that one might use to check one's own ethical/educational action. Here I sketch what each question encourages and enables, centering my comments on quotes from Bailey educators.

"OK, What Do We Have Control Over?": Cultivating the Critical in Response-ability

That there are structural illogics, inequalities, and inequities in public schools and in the communities that create and support them is obvious but requires explicit acknowledgment if educators are to act to enable student growth. For those at Bailey, these could easily have been overwhelming. Located in the American South, Nashville had been the site of racial struggle throughout the 1950s and 1960s and through to the present day.[6] By 2012, there were roughly 120,000 school-aged children in Nashville, but only 80,000 of them—largely Black and immigrant/refugee—attended public schools. Each year, the director of schools went hat-in-hand to the mayor and City Council who had a vested interest in keeping taxes low to suit the white elite (who were putatively liberal but whose children often attended private schools). The Tennessee State Legislature seemed to take pride in underfunding education statewide, but enjoyed especially making things difficult for the Democratic bastions in Nashville and Memphis. The Bailey scholars came largely from Cayce Homes, a sprawling federal housing project located two miles from the school, and brought with them housing and food insecurity. In other words, programs were underfunded, teachers were not well-compensated, and the gentrifying white community around Bailey did not want "other people's children" in their neighborhood.

Educators have no choice but to acknowledge what is, and seek ways to respond educatively in the face of circumstances they do not control. This doesn't mean giving in to inequities or avoiding direct political action, quite the contrary, but it does mean naming them and incorporating that reality into decision-making. Those working toward Bailey's success quickly came to understand that wishing, whining, and willful ignorance earned them nothing, certainly not the attainment of their goal, to educate roughly 400 middle schoolers. Eventually, the students learned the same pragmatist lesson: figure out what *can* be done that will make a limiting situation better now, and in the future, and respond accordingly. In Chapter 4, I highlight how various players came to understand and accept that their capacity to respond to challenging circumstances for the good and growth of students was far greater (in scope and impact) than they anticipated, while also more modest than they might have wished.

"We Can Make Mistakes and We Can Fix Them?": Interpreting and Responding in Community

The critical pragmatist ethic of response and responsibility that came to be standard operating procedure at Bailey proved to be both flexible and effective in addressing very real systemic and pedagogical challenges, immediate and long-range. As an *experimental* mode of proceeding, it is deceptively simple, captured in the phrase, "interpret-respond." It involves an eyes-wide-open acknowledgment of potentially inequitable and seemingly un-generative situations, an embrace of uncertainty and a capacity to stay open, a willingness to bring principles for action and research findings to bear on understanding what's going on, a practice of taking data seriously as one more way of coming to know students, the time and space to imagine and entertain a range of actions-in-response, the ability to anticipate the consequences of each possibility in the light of shared values (and ongoing valuation), the willingness to commit to action, and to reconstruct habits of practice in the light of actual outcomes—and to do this in the context of communities of collaboration. Dr. Sawyer's dramatic change of direction, described in the opening paragraphs of this book, is an example of exactly this, and the staff followed his lead.

In 2015, the National Education Association leadership came to town. Becky Pringle, then NEA vice president and now president, visited Bailey to learn about and highlight the model of teacher leadership that Sawyer imagined and the teacher leaders made real. As part of that visit, a panel of the Bailey teacher leaders explained their work. Greta Knudsen, a science team lead in fifth and sixth grade responded to a question about the distinctiveness of the leadership model with a statement so bold in its directness and simplicity, I will not forget it. Greta said, "We can make mistakes and we can fix them." This is an interpret-respond sentiment I heard over and over again in my interviews with Bailey staff.

"That Was the Expectation": Attending to Relation and Responsiveness

A mode of interpret-respond, no matter how critically and thoroughly practiced, is focused on openness to the situation, including openness to re-describing and redefining the situation itself. Also required for educative experience—and a source of similar uncertainty—is openness to the other, that is, the careful enactment of attention to each other (á la Murdoch) and the responsiveness that goes with it. Only then can both educators and students grow in the capacity to respond, in response-ability. With respect to this element, I focus on the ways communities of collaboration at Bailey were created to include teacher leader, teachers, special educators, paraprofessionals, and residents (with the support of a schoolwide "culture team") to increase and enhance "relational capacity." This relational capacity provided educators with the time and emotional bandwidth to *jointly* offer greater responsiveness to students and their needs and interests. They could attend with care and with engrossment to some scholars, knowing that other members of the team were able to care for other scholars. They could hold scholars to high academic standards, knowing that other members of the team were providing the material and emotional conditions for doing well. The result was that more scholars were seen, encouraged, and challenged in personally meaningful ways, came to trust their teachers and themselves, and, in the process, became responsible to themselves and to the reasonable expectations of their teachers. That both recognition and trust are critical features of educational growth for all students, but especially those who live in conditions of insecurity, is an important truth conveyed and confirmed in the experience of the Bailey community described in Chapter 4.

Within the structure of teaming, individual Bailey educators regularly practiced the kind of attention that Murdoch called for. Principal Sawyer was at the front door every morning, shaking hands and chatting with scholars as they entered the building. He asked teachers to be at the doors of their classroom, modeling the same kind of interaction, and quickly that became the norm. Eventually, other leaders came to the front door in the morning, so that if Sawyer were not there, scholars were still greeted regularly. Each was *seen* as they entered the building.

Counselor April Roberts told me that when she was at Bailey, she knew everybody on the faculty and staff—and sought to know as many scholars as possible. As she put it, "that was the expectation." It is worth noting that the expectations that were most palpable were expectations not about performance or even results, but about relation.

"Let's Remember Who We Are": Making and Taking Responsibility

Each morning, the Bailey community responded together to Dr. Sawyer's prompt, "Let's remember who we are" with "Individuals of character, scholars for life, leaders now and tomorrow." This was a call for scholars, individually and collectively, to take the responsibility that was being offered to them. Initially, as math team leader Karen Dorris told me, "I could tell by their faces that they didn't really believe in it," but by the end of her time at Bailey, the kids recited the pledge every day. "They really were scholars for life."

While largely aspirational in the first year of the experiment, by the second and third years, as the mode of interpret-*respond* and the manner of attention and *responsiveness* took hold, this claim became a counter-narrative of truth-telling, one that belied the social status of the Bailey scholars (and the reputation of the school) as they reconstructed themselves as *responsible* actors. The responsible actor is the person who can look back to look forward, who can account for past histories of association, present situations, and imagined futures to understand oneself as good [teacher, student, person, partner, collaborator, ancestor]. This is where the distinction between responsibility drawn educationally, as a function of growth, and accountability drawn in religious and political terms as a function of blame and punishment, becomes critical.

"We Can Do It . . . But Now*?": Embracing Uncertainty and Staying Open*

In the next chapter, I emphasize the structure and practice that marked Bailey in the light of both contemporary cries that "the sky is falling" and prescribed (and scripted) solutions to the very real challenges facing teachers in schools. I highlight the ways in which the practice at Bailey (1) acknowledges the reality of "the sky is falling" narratives regarding systemic racism, opportunity gaps, inequitable funding, test score declines, etc. but nonetheless (2) confirms *and* exceeds recommendations for "good schools." I point to how structures (like supportive teaming) and infrastructures of norms, attitudes, and affects make it more likely that educators could remain optimistic enough to stay open and embrace the uncertainty that is inherent in the human project that is education.

Both staff and scholars at Bailey knew the "uncertain certainty" that test scores cast over their work and their fate from the beginning. Somehow, with the support of their teams and leaders Sawyer and Jasper, they managed to keep their eyes on the prize of student growth in spite of that shadow. But this became especially difficult in the third year of Sawyer's tenure when the School Improvement Grant was winding down and the progress, though substantial, wasn't enough to hold the "reconstituted school" wolves at bay. The future of both the school and Principal Sawyer was up in the air.

Still, as staff members told me, they knew they could demonstrate the progress needed, but weren't sure if they could do it *now.* And eventually that wasn't good enough, not for them in light of the responsibility they already accepted for scholars' growth, nor for state officials (including charter school advocates) who were hoping to take over at Bailey. In the face of this uncertainty, they persisted.

"Training Wheels" for Response-able Decision-Making

My intention here is not prescriptive and normative, but descriptive and naturalistic. Responsibility (and morality as well) comes to be and is recognizable as a result of interaction, not prior to it. Still, I show here that a critical pragmatist ethic of responsibility does not avoid principles, consequences, or virtues (the building blocks of traditional moral theories), but acknowledges the potential role of each and all of these elements in constructing the meaning of moral action.

In the following, I lay out that model of response-ability that can be developed and refined as a way to practice education with responsibility at its core. I acknowledge that the model described later and the framing offered earlier will not answer any particular ethical or moral query. Only agents in community can do that. Rather, the two serve jointly in a heuristic capacity, that is, as helpful tools to aid ethical deliberation when usually reliable habits fail.[7]

The help of heuristics can be powerful, both for responding in the moment and for reconstructing habits to be employed down the line. Having a heuristic makes it less likely that one will be stymied completely, paralyzed into inaction. Prompted by the heuristics I offer here, we are moved to expand our sights, to pay attention to what is uncovered with a critical but constructive sensibility, to entertain options beyond the readily available—until this very willingness to think it out again becomes a habit of mind, heart, and body. And even then, even the habit of opening up to the new may be reconstructed when the impacts harm relations and impede growth.

As a model for proceeding, what I offer is deceptively simple, captured in the phrase, "interpret-respond," (Niebuhr, 1963) and tested again and again by the extent to which it accomplishes shared educational goals. It is modeled on what Dewey describes in *How We Think* (1910/1980) and *Human Nature and Conduct* (1922/1980), and is rooted in educational interaction in an admittedly inequitable world. It is a "thick" and critical description of what we are already doing whether we acknowledge it or not—for the purposes of making that practice better.

Although I list these elements as sequential moments as if this process moved step by step, in actual lived experience, all moments are occurring at once in a looping circuit that makes meaning possible. Still, when just beginning to check the process and progress of one's own deliberation, it can be helpful to attend to one step at a time.

One further caution: This model is drawn in such a way that it might seem to privilege the individual as a thinker. I address that point directly at the end of the chapter. For now, I will say only this. We experience thinking as individual persons and acts as individual agents (even when collective in character), but that is an illusion, as Dewey documents in *How We Think*. Habits and possibilities of thought and action are socially constructed. This does not obviate the possibility of agency, but that agency is situated in communities of thought and action. Response-ability is linked to the quality of personal decision-making, but also of relational interaction, of group functioning, and of institutional structures. It may be understood as capacity for being and becoming better in specific situations, of responding richly in situations only partly of our own making, and in the process, recreating the conditions for future response and responsiveness. It is an ethic that is consonant with educational efforts and intentions.

Recognition

Much of the time—in education and in all other domains of our lives we rely on past (successful) practice or habit. Consider, for example, how parents assume that their own experience should guide their children's education. That's (mostly) a good thing because it preserves time and energy as we face a life filled with decisions. This can feel especially necessary (though particularly dangerous) in precarious times when anxiety runs high. Sometimes, affective and cognitive dissonance (in the form of internal confusion or external resistance) causes us to realize that our typical actions aren't going to serve us well in a particular situation, either because we battle internal intuitions, or because our habits battle what others take for granted. Sometimes, we actually act out of our own habit, fail miserably to achieve equilibrium (or peace), and are forced to reconsider, to think "outside the box" of the problem itself. It can be an abrupt shift of horizon, what Gadamer refers to as being "pulled up short" (Gadamer, 1998: 268; see also Kerdeman, 2019), or a less crisis-like but still arresting interruption. This is the moment when thinking kicks in.

Now neither failure nor dissonance necessarily means that a habit has no value. It may mean that our timing is off, that we misinterpret some aspect of the situation, or that we encounter another for whom our habits are alien. It may be that this is a particularly novel or especially "wicked" situation. But it certainly means that some new or additional consideration is needed. This is an interruption in the flow of life, but it is a necessary and constructive interruption. The practice of well-formed habits is punctuated by moments of (ethical) deliberation in a life well-lived.

At Bailey, it was the students who sounded the alarm in the form of failing trust and lack of interest in the lessons being offered. Math teacher Madison Knowe noted,

> Our students just didn't let us get away with the textbook . . . If I brought in a worksheet, there was just a riot. It wasn't an option to do something 'normal,' sitting in rows, staring at the board. The curriculum was student-centered by necessity. What do the students want to learn? And how do we get them to hook into it.

Together building leaders, teacher leaders, teachers, specialists, residents, and paraprofessionals were forced to figure out how and what to teach to ensure that the scholars saw themselves in instructional activities. That habit—a willingness to give up the tried-and-true in the face of new evidence and new circumstances—is what prevents educators from getting stuck in tenacity (my way or the highway), authority (anything and anybody to relieve me of the burden), or intuition (abstract analysis can get me where I'm going) (Peirce, 2006).

This willingness to reconsider everything from daily practices to deeply held values (but never all at once!) reveals a recognition that one's actions are always a response to a socially constructed world (and an immediate situation) only partly of our own making, that our control is limited but still substantial, and that the situation demands *our* (individual and collective) careful attention and interpretation. It's a habit that was built into the structure at Bailey, *not* by policymakers, but by educators on the ground. Eventually, it became part of business as usual.

Interpretation

Once we have stopped to consider, to deliberate, that is, once we acknowledge and accept the interruption, interpretation is needed. Put simply we ask, what is going on here? What is the source of dissonance and resistance? Why does past practice not (continue to) produce human flourishing?

In asking this question, we frame the "problem." And care is required, for the way the problem is framed will dictate possible options for action. The needed interpretation may demand micro-, meso-, and macro-analyses, a careful look at interaction, infrastructure, and structures. It's here that critical awareness of cultural and social systems, attunement to affects being negotiated, and loving regard for persons are all indispensable.

And these are precisely the elements that moved Dr. Sawyer to rethink *everything* at Bailey in a remarkable demonstration of "active open-mindedness."[8] As he became acquainted with scholars and teachers, as he understood more about what these young people experienced in their community, as he remembered what he knew about education and politics in Nashville, as he experienced his own frustration and that of everyone around him, and as he clung relentlessly to his belief in the brilliance of the Bailey scholars, he was able to identify what was going on. The school was simply not designed for the flourishing of this student population. Sawyer had to rethink everything. He didn't do that alone but with critical friends and teammates.

In order to earn the descriptor "critical," interpretation requires what Barbara Appelbaum (2022: 55) calls "vigilantly vulnerable informed humility." Without this, it is too easy to short-circuit interpretation by proclaiming innocence under the guise of ignorance. What Appelbaum points to with respect to white complicity in racism can be invoked for all kinds of complicity in social injustice. Because the end here is educational action that is both truly educational and actually ethical through and through, good intentions and voluntary actions are both potentially problematic.

It is also here that ethical and educational principles can be employed not as rules to be obeyed but as valuable social and individual guidelines to be interrogated. It is right to bring consensus notions of what "ought" to be done to bear in the interpretation of the situation, but it is not right to allow "ought" statements to control without further interpretation.

None of this can be accomplished without loving attention, the kind that Iris Murdoch pointed to as a mark of the moral actor.

Anticipation

When interpretation is as thorough as time, circumstances, and self-understanding allow, we turn to possible options for action. This requires the openness to (until-now-unconsidered) options and the capacity to weigh options against likely outcomes. It is here that deontological principles leave off and anticipated (utilitarian) consequences take over.

But before mentally rehearsing anticipated consequences, it is particularly important to think expansively without being bound by the binary choices that so often mark normative ethical arguments. Options for action can and should be imagined, even exhausted, before weighing which is the most fitting response in this situation.

This is what happened at Bailey when Claire Jasper was hired as chief of culture, and she was given the autonomy and budget to create a culture team. Dr. Jasper didn't choose imposed order (needed in hallways and classrooms to ensure a safe and effective learning environment) *or* loving, restorative justice (in order to halt the school-to-prison pipeline). She chose "creative integration" (Follett, 1995) and designed a structure and selected a team whose talents and roles would reinforce both. Deans of students responded to teachers' calls for disciplinary support but arrived not to take scholars away but to support teachers as they brought recalcitrant or uncooperative students back into the fold, sometimes by reconsidering their own role in prompting scholars' resistance. Social workers, counselors, and specialists worked with teacher teams to ensure in advance that student needs were seen and addressed.

Now, of course, options cost more or less, take longer or shorter to enact, require other sacrifices, and offer other rewards. All this is part of the deliberation that is only partly calculable. But again, as with ethical principles in the previous interpretive moment, that calculus is not "the answer." It informs one's decision to act, absolutely. But the calculus is not the decision. Only persons deliberate into action in the context of community.

Communit(ies) of Action

While the recognition of an ethical challenge that calls forth response may be personally or societally based, the interpretation of the situation and anticipation of consequences phases are transacted always in the context of one or more communities of action and value. This is both a challenge to thorough interpretation and a consolation against isolation. I may be bound by familial, religious, cultural, or regional ties, for example, and those ties come with values more or less set, at the same time that new values (and processes of valuation) emerge for consideration and validation. But again, those values—and the virtues embodied in the habits that accompany them—must be uncovered and acknowledged, but do not decide the matter at hand. They inform that decision without question, but in the end, as former US president George W. Bush said about the war in Iraq, ironically it now seems, "I am the decider." It seems that Bush made that statement to claim political power in a situation in which he was, in fact, powerless. The import is different as I construe it here. I am the decider because, as Sartre and deBeauvoir remind us, the decision *becomes me*. It is not political power at stake, but the power to be (me) in the world, a me deeply embedded in my relation to others.

The Bailey teachers' response to the pressures of state testing stands as an example of their capacity to take on the consequences of their decisions about curriculum and instruction. As a school community—including all from the principal to the support staff—these educators chose student growth and trusted that test scores would follow rich and interesting instruction. Improved test scores didn't happen immediately and the "motivational" comments from district and state officials (who thought the teachers didn't understand the stakes perhaps?) didn't help. But the Bailey community, in it together for the well-being of the scholars, stuck to their vision for success. Their self-understanding as educators required it.

No blame or punishment externally imposed was needed. When the district made the decision to close Bailey despite substantial progress that met the state requirements, the teachers rejected this decision as simply wrong. It had no impact on their understanding of their choices and their actions. They knew that they had in good faith exhausted their capacity to interpret and anticipate, and enact what was fitting in that moment and circumstance. That is the burden of responsibility—and, while it may not feel good all the time, it is an experience integral to human beings and educational possibility.

Reconstruction

And so we act, individually and/or in concert.[9] We decide what response best fits the situation by acting, and that action is the indicator of our individual or communal determination. It is the conclusion of a practical argument always situated in the context of social relations and understandings. But any action taken is not the end of the model; it is not a final moment in a sequence but a prompt for further reflection and either a return to (new) habit or further interpretation, anticipation, and response. As we connect action with actual rather than likely consequences—including the responses of those we take seriously and care for and about, we are pushed to make a judgment about that action, about whether the outcome represents flourishing as we understand it—and if it does not, to ponder where we went astray in interpretation and anticipation. If the new response "fits," it is likely that it will result in a new characteristic reaction, that is, a new habit. In Dewey's parlance, habits are reconstructed.

And the pattern of habit and response/reconstruction begins again. As this pattern paid off at Bailey, that is, as interactions with others were enriched and their sense of self as educators expanded, what was a heuristic model employed consciously became a mode of being, one requiring no attention at all. That is, it became a constructive habit. Nonetheless, like all habits, this one too can be reconstructed— as I here reconstruct Dewey's original model by incorporating an explicitly critical perspective.

Useful but Dangerous?

In the pragmatist tradition of amelioration rather than moral fixity, the model I outline here is not about getting to a predetermined right or good response, but to a fitting response, one that is at least usefully wrong. That is, even if the response is a mistake, a "take" that has to be repeated to be improved if not perfected, does the action point usefully to richer interpretation and more accurate imagination of and weighing of anticipated consequences? Does it make the situation better? And for whom? These are never-ending questions. In recognizing that, we are taking Appelbaum's "vigilantly vulnerable informed humility" to heart, further deepening our response-ability.

There are potential dangers in this habit of response-ability, mostly linked to getting caught up in one's own head. One might fail to recognize the difference between healthy rethinking and unhealthy perseveration. One might forget that thinking is never solipsistic (i.e., utterly self-referential). We are always thinking with others, both directly in interaction and indirectly, through common language, assumptions, and expectations.

As we shall see in the next chapter, the critical pragmatist ethic of response and responsibility that came to be standard operating procedure at Bailey STEM Magnet Middle School proved to be both flexible and effective in addressing very real systemic and pedagogical issues, both immediate and long-range, and in envisioning educational success.

CHAPTER 4

Response-ability at Bailey

A critical pragmatist framing of responsibility in education does not emerge from theoretical speculation alone. If not embodied and enlivened in richly described practice, the theory is bloodless, denying its own origins in human interaction. That is why I turn to Bailey STEM Magnet Middle School to lend life to the theory, but it is just as true to say that this theory emerges from experience. But it's also wise to remember, as Anton Chekhov (quoted by George Saunders, 2022) insisted, we don't tell a story to specify answers; we tell stories to frame questions accurately. What Bailey presents to us is not prescription but provocation. It is an opening to get the issues around response-ability right.

Between 2010 and 2012, Bailey was designated persistently dangerous by the state of Tennessee and was, quite simply, an academic disaster. In 2012, a new chapter began at Bailey with a change in principal. When Dr. Sawyer arrived on the Bailey campus in July of 2012, he came with high hopes, boundless energy, and unquestioned commitment, but as noted earlier, he didn't even have a key to the building or furniture for his office. The iconic, old building was in less than perfect repair. Bathrooms were uninviting, partly because of deferred maintenance (linked to differential treatment of schools by the private corporation to whom building maintenance had been outsourced) and partly because of students' lack of respect for the property. Gas leaks were a too common occurrence.

Heating units were too noisy to encourage thoughtful student participation. But the building was big, more than big enough for the 400+ students enrolled, and big enough to accommodate comfortably any plan the Bailey team devised.

While many Bailey students lived in Cayce Homes, about two miles from the Bailey building, the building itself sat within a gentrified and almost exclusively white neighborhood in East Nashville. Homes across the street sold for half a million dollars then. The Bailey "scholars"—as Dr. Sawyer and his staff referred to them relentlessly—rode to school on buses that passed through exclusively white neighborhoods. As one young man mentioned to me, the white women walking dogs nearby would not be found in his neighborhood.

Bailey and other schools in the Nashville iZone ("i" for innovation, but perhaps also for improvement) garnered federal School Improvement Grants. These were three-year awards that required that the school be reconstituted at the start (in 2012, hence a new principal) and, if significant positive results were not achieved, reconstituted at the end of the grant in 2015. This is important because it was a sword hanging over the head of the school and principal in the period between 2012 and 2015.

The early days of the 2012 school year at Bailey were marked by positive energy on the part of Sawyer and his inner circle, but cynicism from staff who were staying on and skepticism from students who simply didn't know what to expect from this young white man who was taking over. Things were marginally better as the year began. But it was only the transition from Sawyer's first year to his second that marked the shift to response-ability, as portrayed in the Introduction. In that summer of transition, some faculty and staff left, either because of the clearly increased expectations (internally, not just externally) or because the coming focus on teaming did not appeal to them. But the ones who stayed were committed, and they hired others, both white teachers and teachers of color, who shared that commitment and who were willing to be a team in more than name only.

Over the next two years, the work was both draining and joyful as person after person attested in the 60+ interviews I conducted with Bailey teachers, leaders, staff, students, and family members. It was two steps forward and one step back on a regular basis.

But there was unquestioned progress on many fronts, enough to make believers out of both faculty and scholars. Claire Jasper posted this on Facebook in 2014, after her first full year as chief of culture:

> I cannot express the profound gratitude I feel for being entrusted with the monumental task of transforming the culture of a school with such a historically dismal reputation! I am humbled to say we did it! Humbled because I have a team of dedicated passionate professionals who caught the vision, and a visionary leader who believed I could get the job done! 70% decrease in discipline incidents over 2 yrs; 50% decrease in chronic absenteeism; 70% decrease in fights and violent offenses this yr; 40% reduction in [Out of School Suspension]; 94.4% attendance rate (highest in 6 yrs); orderly hallways; scholars engaged in rigorous instruction from top teachers in the district; 100% of our teachers report they work in a safe school (up from 40% 3 yrs ago) . . . can't wait to see the impact on achievement.

So there was both hope and fear in the air by the spring of 2015 as the testing time approached. The teachers knew that they had made a difference in the lives of their students and families, and those students had come to understand themselves as scholars. But their hopes would be quashed, not by failure but by something more demoralizing.

The three sections that follow probe the ways that response-ability was practiced and honed continually at Bailey, especially in the two-year period when Drs. Sawyer and Jasper led the effort together. Each section focuses on one of the three domains of educational responsibility: design decisions by policymakers and leaders, pedagogical practices by educators, and goals for students. Those sections are structured to describe examples of each of five marks of a critical pragmatist ethic of responsibility laid out in Chapter 3: cultivating the critical, interpretation and response, relation and responsiveness, making and taking responsibility, and embracing uncertainty and staying open.

Edu-political Responsibility: A Principle of Design

When Hannah Arendt used the term "responsibility" with regard to education (in The Crisis in Education in 1954: 8), she was not talking about responsibility *for* children's development, something we will take up as pedagogical responsibility in the next section. She was talking about responsibility for *the world*, and she was pointing directly to what the new among us (newly born, newly immigrated) bring to any society or particular culture. It is the new, as she articulates with a principle of natality, that has the capacity to save the world from ruin. But Arendt was smart enough to understand that the new doesn't replace the old wholesale but revivifies it, to use Jane Addams' (1907) term. If we choose to educate, we are accepting responsibility for the world.

Who is the "we" who has to make this decision? It is not educators per se but public officials (i.e., federal and state legislators and school board members), educational leaders (e.g., superintendents and building principals), and taxpayer-voters who exercise "edu-political response-ability." They design the system after determining whether there will be a system and who benefits from it. They determine the system's goals and outcomes through the programs they structure and support.

In my lifetime, extending from kindergarten in 1957 until the education of my grandchildren today, policymakers and sometimes administrators in the United States have sought to make the truly difficult task of educating seem simple. They have designed a system as if teachers were technicians who could enact with fidelity the findings of researchers or curriculum experts. The net result—via No Child Left Behind, Race to the Top, and the corollary state systems—has been to narrow the curriculum, constrain the opportunities for school students to explore and create, and to chase the very best educators—the ones who "get" the difficulty and are attracted by the challenge—out of the classroom.

Can responsibility (as response-ability) serve as a robust principle for school and instructional design to reverse this trend? That is, if legislators, school board members, district administrators, and taxpayers keep response-ability in the forefront of their deliberations, will their decisions be more defensible? The educators and scholars at Bailey suggest yes, even as their own policymakers failed them.

Cultivating the Critical

In the Bailey Middle School universe, nearly all the members of the Tennessee Assembly and Senate, the governor, the State Department of Education, and the leadership of the school district were white and male. Coincidentally or not, education was not then and is not now great in Tennessee generally.[1] It seemed obvious to me, as a transplanted Northerner, that funding schools fully and equitably was not a priority—perhaps because most advantaged white students were in Christian academies. For the State Legislature, this was intentional. The district seemed more intent on keeping well-off white families in the district by offering academic magnet schools that would always be majority white. Outside of those magnets, the district worked hard to meet the needs of students with disabilities and English Learners, but sparse funding from both state and city made living up to those commitments difficult. The plight of Black students generated criticism of the students and their teachers, but little internal critique of the structure and organization of district offerings. But that didn't stop the new principal from acknowledging Bailey's social realities.

Christian Sawyer had been a teacher in the district for a decade and had even won a District-wide Teacher of the Year Award when he taught at a high school in a "good" (read white, well-off) neighborhood. When he arrived at Bailey, he brought a critical lens, a willingness to see the material conditions that grabbed the Bailey scholars and held them down. The conditions he saw included public housing in which drug dealing and shootings were commonplace, food insecurity, learning loss grounded in systemic failure, parents who ranged from very motivated and connected to utterly overwhelmed, some holding multiple jobs or parenting from prison. Against the background of consistent achievement failures, these social factors pointed to a need for care for students, what we now call trauma-based instruction, restorative practices, and attention to the school-to-prison pipeline. What remained unquestioned was the talent of the scholars.

Interpretation and Response

I have already noted that interpretation and response don't preclude errors. In his 2012 rush to get Bailey up and running, Sawyer hired a chief organizational officer, a STEM coordinator, a literacy coach, a math coach, and a dean of students. They were all white. Whitney Bradley Weathers, who was to become a central figure in Bailey's transformation, described to me what she encountered when she interviewed at Bailey in the spring of 2013: "a Black school run by white people."

It didn't take long—and it wasn't a tough interpretive challenge—to acknowledge that the Bailey kids needed a critical mass of teachers and leaders that looked like them. Recruiting promising educators of color became a priority, but positions had to be vacated in order to hire anew. Ironically, perhaps, the plan of teaming and teacher leadership that Sawyer was hatching caused some to leave of their own accord.

The district was generally not as willing to challenge business as usual and jump into potentially disruptive interpretations and responses. However, there are two exceptions that paid off.

Just one district official clearly interpreted the distinctiveness of the challenge in the iZone schools, its director, Alan Coverstone. Coverstone responded by extending autonomy for the principals to develop structures supporting teacher leadership. That was a boon for Bailey.

One earlier district response—to a surplus of Race to the Top money[2] in 2010—also supported the habit of interpretation and response at Bailey in a substantial way. In 2010, the district came to Vanderbilt to negotiate a free master's degree for both novice and experienced teachers who would agree to teach in priority schools, Teaching and Learning in Urban Schools (TLUS). The program had a critical lens because that's what Vanderbilt brought, *not* because that's what the district wanted. The district wanted teachers who wouldn't shrink from the most difficult teaching situations and who would increase students' test scores. Vanderbilt delivered that along with a heaping dose of critical perspective and a focus on equity.

Attending to Relation and Responsibility

Attention to relation is where Christian Sawyer shone, obvious in the structure that he created: teaming, teacher (and decentralized) leadership, a restorative, culturally sustaining, and trauma-aware culture, a curriculum that provided challenge and support, and an "everybody's learning" expectation. At Bailey, teaching was a team sport.

Two important structural features marked teaming at Bailey from the beginning: (1) there was less administration and more interaction, more adults deployed on teams to ensure that every child was seen, encouraged, and challenged; and (2) there was a practice of institutional flexibility. When evidence (data about kids' learning, about teachers' satisfaction, and about parents' interest) warranted it, the Bailey folks were ready to go where Murdoch's loving attention led them and pragmatically alter their plans and structures, virtually instantaneously.

Both students and teachers felt supported. Charlsie Wigley, a novice eighth-grade English/Language Arts teacher who spent three years at Bailey, reinforced this point.

> Bailey was the first time I [understood] second-hand trauma, absorbing the . . . trauma that those you care about are experiencing. I'm a fixer, I want to make it better, but if you don't have strong, healthy boundaries, you can pay the price. I experienced that. But I also think the amazing thing was such a strong support network within the school, [colleagues] who knew that about me and gave me the support to be my best self for kids.

Because of this kind of supportive, relation-based structure, teacher wellness went up, sick days went way down, and substitute teachers were never needed. The presence of Vanderbilt residents swelled the relational capacity of the school.

Perhaps the most important (infra)structural element of all is that the teams *included* the scholars. The students at Bailey weren't the objects of instruction, but participants, subjects in their own learning. Teaming wasn't something the teachers did for the kids, but something that the school community constructed together, driven always by who the scholars were, what they cared about and were interested in, and what they needed to learn and grow.

Making and Taking Responsibility

The TLUS partnership with Vanderbilt invited the half-dozen participating Bailey teachers to view data generally (whether from standardized instruments or teacher-devised mastery checks) as a tool to be used to shape instruction rather than as a cudgel of accountability. Data weren't something to be feared, but something to be gathered to confirm habitual action or to enable interpretation and response. Those teachers shared their thinking and their language with their teammates—and that attitude spread, in large part because the structure encouraged that constructive and just-in-time use of data for purposes of instruction rather than student, school, or teacher ranking.

The point is that Bailey was designed with a full acceptance of the staff's responsibility for the well-being and flourishing of the scholars (as future citizens, economic actors, and friends and neighbors). The staff knew they needed to produce evidence of their success. Sometimes they chaffed under the pressure of the highly formalized indicators but, for the most part, they welcomed the responsibility to generate and respond to data because it was built into their professional capacity to do so. Fifth-grade math teacher Kristin Petrony confirmed that:

> As difficult as a population we had at Bailey, that was probably one of my least stressful years [as a teacher] because I was able to focus on what was important. Karen [Dorris, team leader] was able to support me with a lot of the other things. All teachers know we need to analyze data, we know we need to stay on top of our grades, we know we need to contact parents, we know we need to do all these things. We are limited by time and being just one human. Having [Dorris] as a partner teacher along with being a coach made all the difference in the world.

Embracing Uncertainty and Staying Open

A bureaucratically formed educational institution focuses on management rather than leadership, replaces education with efficiency and economic effectiveness, establishes hierarchical relations as normative, and privileges "impartial" rule enforcement over situationally informed judgment. In other words, bureaucracies don't tolerate uncertainty. Still, in settings where homogeneity cannot be assumed, uncertainty is part of the landscape. In such settings, a different social theory and theory of change is needed, one that recognizes the potential mismatch between leaders, providers, and consumers/clients, that welcomes conflict as an opportunity for communication and growth.

Ironically, by creating the iZone—on paper intended to bring failing schools up to snuff, Metro Nashville Public Schools offered more autonomy to its failing schools than it did to its other schools. But with failing status and the accompanying autonomy came a large measure of uncertainty. Yes, you can make decisions as a school, but make a misstep and the school will be closed.

The Bailey team understood both the double-edged system of accountability they were working in and the uncertainty built into the lives of Bailey students and worked to respect those realities. Most of all, they acknowledged the uncertainty of their own status as well-intentioned and skilled educators who might nevertheless "fail," at least in the eyes of those external constituencies who stood to judge them. They navigated that uncertainty by staying open to learning from the scholars and each other, by challenging habits with equity in mind, and by replacing hierarchies with distributed responsibility and collaboration.

Pedagogical Responsibility: Guide for Educational Practice

Even as the staff at Bailey accepted the things they could not change, they stayed focused on the "We can . . . ," and found they could imagine multiple responses. They were not stuck on either test scores or student interest but recognized that student flourishing required both. Children were not either gifted or "behind." They were all in need of both focused assistance and interesting challenge. They did not get caught in a dichotomy between (stifling) order and (productive) chaos but realized that "order" could be understood through interest and activity for plenty of productive effort and a healthy dose of unstructured chaos. They didn't understand their scholars as good or bad, traumatized or untouched, but always as growing and in need of both guidance and restoration. They came to accept that their capacity to respond to challenging circumstances for the good and growth of students was far greater (in scope and impact) than they anticipated while also more modest than they might have wished. And it was greater when acting collaboratively and in concert.

Cultivating the Critical

To cultivate the critical is not to engage in retrospective responsibility, to blame others for their failings. It is not simply to point to what is wrong with the systems shaping and limiting our interactions. Rather, it involves taking a hard look at how things are, questioning both how they got that way and whether they have to be that way. This isn't easy because it means taking a look at oneself in the context of what is taken for granted in your communit(ies) of action and identity. Bailey teachers experienced this over and over.

When Whitney Bradley actually started teaching at Bailey, her careful attention yielded a new insight: Black leaders were in culture positions and white leaders in academic positions. This too sent a potentially problematic message, even if particular leaders were in the right positions to maximize their interests and talents. Bradley continued to speak up, to point to patterns of staffing that warranted continued attention. She did not have the autonomy or authority to fire and hire new people, nor did she want to fire valued white colleagues or override others' ability to shape the hiring for their teams. What to do?

Bradley was a critical disruptor, recognizing that a circumstance had become a problem—even if others didn't see it. Both the habit of hiring the "most qualified person for the job," or worse, the habit of assuming that Black educators can connect personally with Black children but may not be well suited to teach them needed to be disrupted at Bailey, so that interpretation and response, not reaction, can occur.

Bradley's disruption, her insistent but not obnoxious observation that race needed to be a hiring consideration—for the sake of the Bailey scholars and the growth of the staff—created a sense of need and an appropriate sense of urgency, at least in some quarters. Over time, a new normal (a new habit) came to be, one in which *of course* assumptions were checked and candidates of color were actively sought (though not presumed the most qualified) for all positions. Interpretation and response gave way to a new habit of action.

Interpretation and Response

At Bailey, students and teachers alike were encouraged to "take a shot." Failure wasn't something to be feared but a step on the path to understanding and growth. The shots the educators took were not shots in the dark. They were well-considered, often collaborative, always data-informed, and rooted in the real circumstances, gifts, and cultural histories of the Bailey scholars and the teachers themselves. It is just this that makes them responsible decisions, shots that will work or, at least, reshape the next shot.

Almost immediately, teacher teams came to realize that their newly realized team capacity for grouping students for optimal learning presented ongoing challenges. Grouping by apparent ability or skill level or even who got along with whom often did aid learning *for some students*, but wasn't generating the kind of learning atmosphere they sought. They didn't just want good results; they wanted great results and they weren't getting them. This dissatisfaction led to speculation about why the usual strategies were not working better and prompted round after round of interpretation and response: patterns of mastery linked to groupings, teacher observations of social interactions, research findings with respect to grouping for equity, and different sized groups based on student need. On two different teams, sixth-grade math spearheaded by Karen Dorris, and eighth-grade literacy, pushed by residents Amanda West and Andrea Clifford, the teams independently—and at different moments—came to the option that splitting groups by gender might address some of the (usually temporary) social interactional issues that were distracting the scholars. They worked with colleagues and parents to change student grouping—and reported impressive results in terms of documented learning, but also, and importantly, in terms of the climate for learning the single-sex grouping made possible. In the sixth grade, it was the girls who benefited enormously, with Dorris enthusiastic about "crazy success" in a move that helped the young women and did not hurt the young men. In the eighth grade, West described the incredible calm that these rapidly growing young men experienced in being able to read quietly without what was, for them, the distraction of young women. These boys (still boys despite rapidly maturing bodies) were learning to be students once freed from the demands of posturing that growing up heterosexual required.

The pedagogical response-ability these teachers practiced in implementing these time-bound experiments paid off—for themselves and their students in those settings. Single-sex grouping became one more pedagogical action that might be employed when circumstances called for it.[3]

Attending to Relation and Responsibility

Christian Sawyer stood at the front door every day and paid attention. Counselor April Roberts knew everybody (all the staff and most of the students), because "that was the expectation." Students were unfailingly referred to as "scholars," a habit that enabled them to know that they were seen, encouraged, and challenged.

The link between relation and responsibility was built into both structure and ethos at Bailey as I have pointed out, but it's important to highlight the power of attention. Even when we practice habits that value relation, it is too easy to allow those habits to become rote. As Iris Murdoch reminds us, moral sensitivity and perception are implicated in both interpretation and response.

I was privileged to observe team meetings regularly, meetings in which teachers checked (local and standardized) data against their own perceptions and the perceptions of others on the team to consider and determine the next steps. The attention that was lavished on the needs of individual students was impressive. And that attention came from and led back into the quality of relations that made making and taking responsibility possible.

Janita Sanders was a special educator at Bailey serving seventh- and eighth-grade students in math and science settings. I talked with her at length about the attitude toward and practice of inclusion at Bailey. In her words,

> I remember sitting [in teams] discussing high risk kids, trying to figure out which adult was the best adult to attend to whatever was going on . . . Those were really special times. I had never been in a school system that took that extra time to really get child specific, took the time to get to know everybody, not just the "frequent flyers."

Making and Taking Responsibility

The phrase "taking responsibility" has a dominant valence associated with being willing to "man up" (the gender reference here is intentional) and recognize one's role in causing some mishap. Blame or sanction is expected. (One is rarely urged to take responsibility for a spectacular success. Interestingly, that's a question of "credit" rather than responsibility.) This is the state of affairs a critical pragmatist ethic of responsibility seeks to alter, to understand not that we should take responsibility when we screw up, but that we, in our interactions with one another, *make* that responsibility that we are then both willing and able to take. The responsibility we make is tied to the persons (educators) we will and want to be in the world. And the driver of responsibility made and taken by the staff at

Bailey was the attention paid to each and every student, and the shared belief that the students could succeed and flourish and that the educators could, collectively and individually, impact that flourishing positively.

When I asked LeKeisha Harding, a special educator and team leader, to tell me about a moment when she knew her leadership made a positive difference, she described the process that she and her team devised to release Q, a seventh grader, from his special education designation. As those who work with children with special needs in American schools know only too well, it can be an onerous process to get a student qualified for additional instructional support.[4] Unfortunately, it is just as onerous to remove the special education designation when it is no longer useful. For an adolescent male, being labeled "special education" is generally not desirable.

Q had first been labeled in elementary school and there is no way to know in retrospect whether his academic and behavioral struggles were cognitive, maturational, emotional, or some combination. We don't know, for example, whether he was caught in the net of active youngsters (of color) who communicate through call-and-response or who think best when on the move. But by the time he hit seventh grade and his first encounter with Keisha Harding, he was resisting services that required his being pulled out of class. Fortunately, the teaming model at Bailey meant both that he was rarely pulled out and that Keisha, the special education specialist/advocate who worked with him in a thoroughly inclusive setting, became aware that his achievement and behavior compared favorably with his peers. Keisha was positioned to see his real strengths as a communicator and as a leader.

So she formed a partnership with Q and his other teachers to gather the data needed to loosen the label of "special needs." Academic outcome data were supplemented by observing Q in various settings, checking how well he was able to advocate for himself, and seeking feedback from his family about expectations and interactions at home. At the end of a full year of collaborative effort, Q was no longer on the roster of students with special needs. He would finish at Bailey and move on to high school freed of the label he carried as a stigma.

As she spoke, it was clear to me not only that the entire team had a hand in this educative move, but that it was Keisha's practice of leadership—through visioning, data analysis and sharing, and facilitating thoughtful reflection about and with students—that made responsibility for each (and every) team member possible. It was only because all (including Q's family) did their part, that he could step away from a useful but problematic designation that was no longer supporting him.

Embracing Uncertainty and Staying Open

In March of 2015, Christian Sawyer's third year as a principal (and the third year of a federal School Improvement Grant), the Bailey students submitted to state testing. The faculty knew that *these* scores would determine Bailey's fate. If students achieved the designated levels for progress and if they posted significant growth beyond that which was expected, then good things could happen. The school would not be taken over by the state of Tennessee, nor would it be signed over to a charter management organization for conversion. Dr. Sawyer could remain the principal and the staff could retain their jobs. The Bailey scholars would not be scattered by the winds of school evaluation and "reform." Of course, if the test score marks were not hit, any combination of these things would happen.

There was reason to think that progress had been made—and that scores might improve enough to secure the school's future. Prior year results were promising, especially in mathematics, science, and social studies, though reading and writing had been less positive. Still, the energy in the school was good and periodic MAP (Measures of Academic Progress) testing, generally predictive of the summative state tests, suggested that even the literacy scores might rise substantially. But it was not a sure thing, and the temptation to shut down the whole operation in favor of test prep of the worst kind was clear and present.

Dr. Sawyer appeared to be, and the teachers confirmed him to be, a master of keeping the pressure off the teachers and keeping the focus on the growth of the scholars. Everybody knew that the test scores would have real consequences, and teachers talked openly about what kind of preparation might actually support the scholars through the testing, but nobody abandoned their culturally responsive pedagogy nor their focus on what would engage the scholars.

Personal Responsibility: Goal for Students

In the Introduction, I described Bailey scholars' running in the hallway and how their response to collision developed over time, demonstrating their growing capacity to recognize what was happening and respond in ways that privileged caring attention and rich relation, while taking responsibility for oneself. This is not the edu-political responsibility created in institutions or the pedagogical responsibility enacted by teachers in collaboration, but a *personal* responsibility. That responsibility is not, as poet Galway Kinnell (1989) puts it, "merely personal," that is, individualistic, rational, and juridical, but "truly personal," that is, rooted in who one is in community in all its depth of feeling. This personal responsibility can serve as both an objective for teachers' instructional efforts and an indicator of students' educational success.

One immediate, and perhaps understandable, objection might be that "personal responsibility" (even built out in its enactment in interaction as response-ability) is not specific enough to let educators, families, and policymakers know when we have succeeded, when students are educated (or at least as educated as they could or should be at a given point in their lives.) And even if I am willing to say that a student or students have an appreciable capacity to respond to the situations that challenge them in a fitting way (given their age, etc.), is that enough to claim with confidence that we have succeeded in *educating* them?

Consider the assumptions built into this objection, however. We are currently bewitched by the standards movement of the last several decades, a movement that specifies exactly what kids should know and be able to do at a grain size that *can* guide teachers in curriculum planning but that far too often misses the larger goal of education, that is, the integrated ability to read the world, to read oneself, and then to figure out what the world is calling you to contribute. This is exactly what education as response-ability points to. And yet, this is utterly missing in too many public schools, especially those schools that serve children and young folks disadvantaged by race, class, culture, or language. Instead, we dumb down and narrow their curriculum.

Too often, we lose sight of what we actually *want* for our own children and the young of our community. We want them to be good neighbors, good friends, good partners, good employees, good parents, and so on, and we want them to have the capacity to determine what "good" means in each and every interaction. None of the measures currently employed to determine school success even have proxy value for our actual goals. In an educational system where *Someone Has to Fail* (Labaree, 2010), we construct goals that sort rather than grow all our young people.

If one is response-able, that means they can accurately assess the situation, determine "what is," interpret what "what is" means politically, interpersonally, culturally, and so on, imagine defensible options for action and then accurately predict how each of those options will play out, and act in the light of personal and communal values. This does not specify what knowledge is of most worth (here and now) but still demands that one has mastered "school subjects" (concepts and content in literature, history, math, science, languages, arts) *and* that one is capable of dialogic communication of all kinds in order to generate the knowledge useful in the moment.

I turn to the examples offered by Ted Sizer's Coalition of Essential Schools[5]—and Deborah Meier's particularly successful exemplar, Central Park East High School—to demonstrate that a school curriculum can, in fact, prepare students for college and career by conceptualizing success in terms akin to response-ability.[6] To graduate from Central Park East, a student had to prepare fourteen independent projects built around five "habits of mind" that echo a critical pragmatist perspective: evidence, perspective, connections, supposition, and relevance (see Meier, 1995). In this "graduation by portfolio," a portfolio that targeted academic subjects as well as a students' life experience, self-understanding, caring relationships, and future plans, students not only prepared projects and presentations but defended the entire portfolio to a panel of teacher and community members.

With Sizer, Meier, and many other excellent educators, I claim that personal responsibility is *exactly* the right grain-sized goal to let us check progress toward and accomplish growth. It is just enough specification (in the context of a school culture that supports these habits of mind) to motivate and guide educators and to tell us when we have not succeeded.

It is important to state clearly that families of children of privilege, those who attend private schools or well-off public districts, demand exactly this sense of response-ability as the desired outcome for their students. Moreover, they have the wherewithal to get what they want, either by paying tuition (individually) or by supporting high enough property taxes on highly valued real estate (collectively).

Cultivating the Critical

The Bailey scholars had seemingly always known the reality of their own social and economic status, and they knew only too well that they attended a largely Black school in a gentrified and totally white neighborhood. The global literacy curriculum at Bailey had at its core an intention to illuminate this, to lift up scholars' capacity to name their own experience in the world in ways that did not ignore race, class, gender, able-bodiedness, culture, or language. In other words, each scholar learned about themselves by learning about the world they inhabited. But this existential goal was tethered to one concrete reality and two contingent observations. Scholars had generally low levels of basic literacy, so the curriculum at Bailey would need to be literacy intensive to enable these obviously bright youngsters to catch up. But how? Sawyer knew that citizenship mattered at least as much for disenfranchised youngsters as for better-off students, and social studies content offered a text-rich and relevant context for literacy learning. Also, social studies was then a tested subject in Tennessee, and the social studies tests might be easy pickings for some gains. So he didn't choose between more literacy or more social studies; he imagined both literacy and social studies in a mixture he simply called "Global Literacy," a placeholder for something the teacher teams invented day by day, week by week. They opened the Tennessee standards and used them as a reference as they found sets of texts—including but never limited to textbooks. They used short and longer pieces, hard copy and online documents, fiction and nonfiction, prose and poetry (and linked the whole set to images—political cartoons, artworks, and photographs—that could be "read" as well.) With Sawyer's leadership, Language Arts teachers and social studies teachers across four grade levels recognized the need for something different and invented it through collaborative trial, error, and reconstruction over time.

This was impressive in itself, but critical to the success of global literacy were the tasks and assessments that teachers asked of the scholars. They did close readings of texts; they did reading circles; they did online literacy skill work. But that drill and practice operated much like drills at an athletic practice session. The drills were situated within broader tasks that were actual "scrimmages," opportunities for scholars to play the game of response-ability. I note just one example recounted by Vanderbilt residents Kenan Kerr and Julia Konrad working together in eighth grade: "We studied oral traditions of the *griots* in West Africa, and then had students write their own folktales, embedding a theme relevant to life in West Africa and contemporary life in East Nashville." The assessment of these assignments was never focused purely on the skill execution, but always also on the ways students made sense of the task and constructed meaningful responses.

Interpretation and Response

Perhaps the best example of a task that demanded interpretation and response from student participants was not technically academic but very much a part of the ethos of Bailey, the Bailey Beat. The Bailey Beat team had full responsibility for the broadcasting facility that Dr. Sawyer and Ms. Hasfjord managed to put together out of STEM Grant funds and local partners' support. The most frequent use of the video broadcasting capacity involved the daily morning show.

Initially, the Bailey Beat was a rote exercise as participants became familiar with the equipment and the medium of broadcasting. The simple truth is that most of these scholars had never seen this kind of equipment, let alone been encouraged to imagine novel uses for it, so I won't suggest that they became experts. They were, after all, middle schoolers. But over time, these seventh- and eighth-grade scholars figured out together what all this afforded them, and the Bailey Beat interviews became more substantive, the news more provocative. Watching them make that space their own tool for expression and community, watching them develop confidence that this was not outside their sphere of possibility, would convince anyone that they—individually and collectively—were steadily developing response-ability.

Attending to Relation and Responsibility

The capacity to attend to others as persons is a critical element of response-ability and cannot be taken for granted in anybody, student or adult, who has experienced trauma and insecurity (with respect to food, income, housing, etc.) on a regular basis. Too many of the Bailey scholars were not in the habit of viewing adults in their lives as caring resources. Until they could see and acknowledge that others (both peers and adults) were interesting and interested, it would be almost impossible for them to learn and grow in substantive ways.

Without naming it as such, the teams at Bailey were designed to model caring in the sense that Nel Noddings (1983, 1993) laid out in the 1980s in *Caring* and *The Challenge to Care in Schools*. As Noddings limns it, there is "natural caring," but the moral habit of caring as a verb (the habit the Bailey scholars often lacked), involved learning to care for oneself, for intimate others, for distant others, for the natural world, for human-made objects, and for ideas. Implied in this scheme is that robust caring for ideas (e.g., algebraic relations or justice) is dependent on developing other forms of caring, starting close to home.

The Bailey teachers modeled caring as an active practice, and created openings for the scholars to respond as "cared for." Initially, those others included the snake named Bailey that math teacher Madison Knowe kept in her classroom, or the plants in the garden that global literacy teacher Kristyn Boone designed and cultivated with the scholars. It moved on to the members of one's athletic team—in football, basketball, volleyball, and cheerleading. It involved teachers' giving students rides home after an athletic event or delivering food to families in a snowstorm. It could be seen in teachers' taking students' work seriously, and by extension, taking students seriously. Eventually, scholars began to feel that their teachers did care and would care for them. That caring extended to others they saw regularly in the building (like me!) Finally, slowly, one could see that ideas began to matter, not for all students all the time, but for most students at least some of the time. We know that this happened because students told us it did. In a post in summer 2022 on Facebook, long-graduated scholar Yasmine Summers reminded Dr. Sawyer that she loved him because he had loved her and done so much for her and all her peers.

Relational capacity, that is, the time and space for, and valuing of constructive interaction, at Bailey grew over the years of Dr. Sawyer's tenure as principal, and with relational capacity came response-ability. While at Bailey, the students in the seventh grade one year formed a Facebook group called seventh at Bailey. They have stayed in touch and two summers ago they planned a reunion at a Nashville park. The students gathered to enjoy each other, to share news of their lives, and to mourn the death of one of their own in a random and unexplained shooting at a convenience store. These are the things that responsible people do.

Making and Taking Responsibility

In the meantime, the staff at Bailey worked very hard to give students opportunities to practice response-ability in domains where they didn't feel doomed to failure. Dr. Sawyer and STEM teacher Julie Hasfjord implemented STEM electives, mini-courses reflecting a teacher's "passion" that met for an hour one day a week. Scholars chose the elective that interested them or perhaps chose the teacher they wanted to develop a relationship with. The content of the electives ranged from gardening to cooking to fashion to herpetology (yes, the care of snakes!). Sometimes the STEM connection was clear; other times less so. But what was common to all the sessions was greater freedom and autonomy for the scholar participants to engage without fear of failure as they collaborated with at least one teacher and a group of peers.

The Student Council met during the STEM Elective hour. Special Educator LeKeisha Harding worked with the Nashville Science Center to start the Bailey Boutique (a student-run store that "sold" gently used clothing to students who needed it—using Bailey Bulldog Bucks, incorporating alterations and "light up" fashion design). Gokul Krishnan, a Vanderbilt doctoral student who is now an instructional designer of maker spaces in pediatric hospital settings, came over to Bailey to coach a group of students who wanted to create a Makers' Space attached to the school library. The Bailey Beat crew used this time for their planning and rehearsal. In each of these settings, scholars took the lead. Some STEM electives produced interesting results, others were less successful, but, in virtually all, the scholars understood that the activities required their active and thoughtful responses.

Embracing Uncertainty and Staying Open

As I have suggested earlier, none of this was easy, and success—for the teachers or the scholars—was not ensured. What is perhaps most remarkable is that the educators and scholars kept the faith together, in part because teachers "wrapped around" the scholars, reminding them that they were not alone. They hung in there on days when it felt hard, either because district officials disrespected the school and the staff, because some students were acting the fool, or because the trauma in their lives was too present. Their "grit" was not simply a character trait located in individuals, but a function of the social arrangements of recognition, support, and challenge that were intentionally set up. It helped *a lot* that the school found a way to have more smart, committed bodies in the school to share the load. Everybody knew that success was not a sure thing, but the attitude—expressed provocatively by Whitney Bradley Weathers—was "You have *no choice . . .*" The educators who had no choice recognized that the scholars had no choice either. Their lives literally depended on it. The responsibility they created for themselves was a responsibility to the integrity of their own lives.

The ethos at Bailey expressed confidence in the scholars' capacity to do everything any other kids could do. That culture of caring become love nestled in limits, and love, eventually, became learning, because the scholars were invited to make the responsibility that they then took onto themselves. They began to understand that they had some control over who they would be in the world.

Zee Jennings, president of the Student Council in 2014–15, said it clearly. "The teachers at Bailey made us feel like we were top notch, that we were capable of reaching anything." It wasn't just the attention they paid to them, but also what they expected of them. Zee spoke pointedly about how the neighborhood she grew up in "conditioned [her] to be a certain way," but that being at Bailey enabled her to make of herself "the person [she] is today."

Reflecting on Response-ability at Bailey

Reading about teaching and learning at Bailey is not startling or even impressive—until one remembers the current state of practice in schools, the current state of demoralization among teachers, and the current strangling surveillance of public schools. The leaders, teacher leaders, teachers, specialists, residents, paraprofessionals, support staff, *and* students at Bailey all exercised response-ability across a range of challenges and, in the end, *made* the responsibility they accepted for what the school was and how it impacted the lives of those who were part of the community. They also accepted responsibility for how Bailey measured up with respect to test scores not because they believed those scores were a fair picture of their accomplishments, but because they understood that those measures were an important token in the system that would decide whether they could continue to exercise their response-ability in the Bailey setting. It was the latter that mattered to them.

This captures an important point about the distinction between accountability externally imposed and responsibility understood as the dual capacity to respond richly in the context of lived experience and to accept responsibility for one's responses. *If one starts with responsibility as accountability, there is no guarantee that response-ability will be developed or even recognized. But if one focuses on response-ability, the very process leads to making and taking responsibility.* This is not necessarily the status quo accountability that is normatively prescribed by the powers that be, but a responsibility that better fits what the known demands.

Ironically, creating the conditions for the exercise and practice of response-ability seems to return our attention to the elements of responsibility highlighted by Aristotle and Kant (freedom, will, autonomy, agency) *as well as* the modern insights offered by theorists after Nietzsche (relation, response, intelligence, attention). Something like accountability remains but it is a mutual responsibility to each other in community, not a "pay-up" accountability imposed by those who control those who lack power.

CHAPTER 5

Conclusion

My contention here is not that the retrospective view of responsibility as accountability is never useful, but that this view represents a first (and crude) approximation of responsibility in childhood, and later, abstracted, institutional, and power-laden external impositions of responsibility. What it does not represent is the mature experience of response-ability, the capacity to respond as oneself in the world. Maturity demands the *experience* of responsibility, not as external control but as personal (i.e., interactional) response to the world inhabited by others. In short, responsibility is the (acknowledged and accepted) power to choose differently in response to the *past*, at this *present* moment, and for the *future*. This is the view opened up in different ways by the continental philosophers, pragmatists, and British women cited earlier. It is the view lived by the educators and scholars at Bailey. I don't know if any of the Bailey educators ever read Sartre, Levinas, Dewey, or Murdoch, but I do know they acted as if they understood the sense of what those philosophers offer us. They recognized that they were creating themselves as educators through their actions, that they could only do that by acknowledging the relations with students and each other that made them educators, that reconstructing habits of mind, heart, and action required openness and intelligence, that loving attention was the most fruitful place to start. This is, in reality, an option available to all educators, and, I suspect, is already being enacted unconsciously in schools where the people and the conditions are right. My hope is that this book will further the conscious practice of response-ability by more educators in more places.

In the Introduction I asked, how can a school be designed so that *all* persons in it are response-able, being and becoming both smart and good, working toward outcomes that are generative, just, and equitable? This is what happened at Bailey. Response-ability is what made Bailey a good school,[1] but this doesn't match perfectly with how most of us would describe a good school: one great teacher in each classroom; dynamic principal; high test scores; order everywhere; schedules set; curriculum specified; teachers teaching; students learning. Once again, what we take for granted is not quite right.

The Bailey experience suggests that a good school is a place where the boundaries separating classroom spaces are permeable and teachers share responsibility for all students' well-being and achievement; where *everything* in the school is negotiable except the well-being and development of the teachers and students in it; where students know they are cared for and respond by learning to care in return. The good school that was Bailey was a space where all were growing and equity was a constant concern; where each one had a voice and everybody had responsibility, where teachers were leaders, and leaders were always learning. It was, as it could be in any school and is in many more schools than we acknowledge,[2] a site of response-ability powering responsibility in its more-than-accountability sense.

These are lessons worth learning especially now in the face of post-pandemic efforts to address both learning loss and the disorientation that too many youngsters are experiencing as a result of education pursued piecemeal over the past several years. Many of the Bailey scholars had already experienced learning loss and the Bailey team addressed that by "dividing and differentiating," in effect, their own version of small group, high-impact tutoring. But it seems clear, to me and to the scholars and teachers at Bailey, that the personalized instruction was only effective set in the context of teaming, careful attention to each teacher and scholar, and ambitious goals for all. It seems foolish to prescribe any one "silver bullet" to address what is clearly a broader challenge to our educational priorities.

Casey's Death

In the third year of Principal Sawyer's tenure, a singular event occurred: the suicide of an eighth-grade student.[3] This was not a moment of growing dissatisfaction focused into interpretation that yielded possible actions that could be weighed and chosen. This was a moment of being pulled up short, a moment when you realize that your "horizon" of understanding is shifting, and you feel as though you have to react whether you want to or not. The great challenge is to resist reaction until you have sorted through what this event means and what it might mean for faculty and students going forward, to deliberately engage in interpretation and response in the context of this particular community of living and learning.

We know the usual reaction to a student's death in a school. There is a public announcement of the death and an offer of support services to those who are grieving. These are good things, but they can be pro forma rather than responsive. And they offer little to the creation of community that will be altered by loss.

What happened after Casey's death is a model of pedagogical responsibility, understood not as an individual task, but as a collaborative possibility. This model response was possible because the Bailey structure and infrastructure already supported relations of trust, assumptions of collaboration, and the laser-like focus on the well-being of the scholars and of each other. News of this popular student's seemingly inexplicable death was going to rock this little school community, and Sawyer knew it.

So Principal Sawyer talked with team leaders, told them everything he knew, explained that he and Chief Culture Officer Jasper were gathering information, communicating with the district office and with Casey's family, identifying students and teachers who knew Casey well, and formulating a plan that would create community even as the news it carried would cause pain and rupture. He asked the leaders to be sure that all staff members knew exactly what he knew but bound them all to silence until they were ready to share the news with students and with families.

In an almost miraculous occurrence, the word reached all staff but did not leak out to students. Throughout the morning, teachers and others were updated as plans were made. A letter from the principal was composed and distributed to all the teachers. At 1:30 p.m., Principal Sawyer would make an announcement asking scholars to listen to their teachers as they read a letter about some very sad and distressing news. Then teachers would read the same letter to classes all around the building. Teachers communicated with one another throughout the morning about how to group students for optimal support at that hour, who might need greater support, and how to both hold space for students and teach them how to work through this kind of news. All of this communication was possible because Bailey did not operate on a one-teacher, one-classroom eggcrate model. Students were used to seeing teachers moving back and forth, communicating with each other about all sorts of matters. And the extra-relational capacity the teams made possible ensured that no students were "uncovered" while this planning was going on.

So many elements were ripe for interpretation here. Who was Casey and how would his death impact the students? What about the fact of his suicide? How should that be treated? Which teachers would themselves need support and how could they best support their students? How could they share this news in a way that would build up their capacity to live through it? And what might be done? Share it immediately or hold the news knowing it might leak out? Have the principal make the announcement or, recognizing the vagaries of an old PA system, have the news delivered in a more intimate setting? Bring the students to the auditorium in groups? How to let parents know? How to marshal the capacities of counselors and others? How to obtain enough counseling support? There is no way of knowing that the (set of) action(s) you take is the very best action, but rich interpretation in the context of *this* community allowed the staff to make a decision they knew they could live with.

The Bailey community came together in a way that I, as an observer, can only call deeply moving. Kids and teachers cried together. There was no acting out or taking advantage. And the school made it possible for any child and family who wanted to attend the funeral to do so without pressuring anybody to feel something they didn't. An event that was deeply distressing became a rallying point for the development of the school as a learning community because those charged with the education of children (from the custodians and lunch workers to the principal) practiced responsibility.

Pipe Dream or Possibility?

Given the "deformed politics" of the day, is there any chance we can rally around responsibility as a focus for education? Am I just wasting my time by not giving in to the realpolitik of the time? This is an important, worthwhile question that can't be answered fully here. Nonetheless, there are reasons to hold on to a bit of critical pragmatist optimism.[4]

The first reason is that responsibility has broad and immediate rhetorical, ethical, and educational appeal. Nobody is *against* responsibility, socially or morally, individually or collectively. It is not that simple of course. Taking responsibility as response-ability seriously would require a shift in understanding for many of us, even those inclined to find value in my argument. The human reality is that we too often *want* to know at a gut level who else to blame and punish when something goes wrong so that we can defensively deflect blame or complicity from ourselves. But this is an adolescent reaction, not a thoughtful, reasoned, and emotionally aware response. It is the kind of habitual reaction that education should enable us to grow beyond, to reconstruct. My appeal in this book—and the reason I rely so heavily on lived experience at Bailey—is to educators who can recognize and appreciate the compelling nature of practice and the educative power of outcomes that a focus on response-ability enables. If educators appreciate this, they can act, individually and collectively, even within and cognizant of the systems that are currently constraining them. I have little hope of finding a hearing among those who seek political advantage, but every hope that educators are presently hungry for a philosophical framing that allows them to enact the motivations that brought them to education to begin with.[5] I also have faith in parents who ultimately just want what allows their youngsters to flourish.

Still, I want to explicitly acknowledge the enacted fear and existential discomfort that is rampant on all sides of our deformed politics—and may well be the most important obstacle to the educational practice of response-ability across policy, pedagogy, and personal action. It is impossible to understand our inability to communicate across political and educational lines without acknowledging that we have given in to the avoidance and distancing that marks fear. In a pointed *New York Times* piece about the divide that now appears even in late-night television, Tressie Macmillan Cottom (2022) notes that "We are too scared to laugh." Until that changes, I admit that perhaps response-ability is relegated to pipedream. Still, I persist as the Bailey team did.

The second reason for critical pragmatist optimism is that the language of responsibility, understood in a mode congenial to response-ability, is finding a comeback and transformation in both education literature and philosophical attention. Kelly Oliver's theorizing of responsibility in *Response Ethics* (2018) is particularly rich. Michael Gunzenhauser's (2012) *The Active/Ethical Profession: A Framework for Responsible*

Educators and Sarah Stitzlein's (2017) *American Public Education and the Responsibility of its Citizens* both bring the concept of responsibility to bear philosophically on current educational issues and practice. In empirical research related to learning, scholars like Grace Chen, Samantha Marshall, and Ilana Horn (2020) are investigating how teachers make sense of their pedagogical responsibility, examining the pedagogical action (the "what" and "how") of teaching mathematics, as well as the purpose of teaching mathematics (the "why") by exploring the pedagogical reasoning entrenched in pedagogical responsibility.

Critical pragmatism, relationality, and mutual accountability are also easy to find in intellectual and educational speculation. As I sketched briefly in the Introduction, feminist voices, white women and women of color, have, over the past four decades, represented the relationality and responsiveness that earlier theorists cleared space for. Care theorists like psychologist Carole Gilligan (1983) and philosopher Nel Noddings (1983, 1993) gave educators a language for an important element in educational practice. Long before Gilligan and Noddings, Black feminist theorists extending back at least to Anna Julia Cooper (1892/2017)—including Audre Lorde (1984), bell hooks (1994), Pat Hill Collins (1990), Katie Cannon (2006), Emilie Townes (2006) and so many others—could not look away from the relational dimensions of politics, education, and ethics.

The power of this work is especially evident where critical pragmatism and relational understanding collide. I point to Megan Boler's (1999) work and Sara Ahmed's (2003) theorizing on how past histories of association mark how we "feel power." As noted earlier, New Materialists Karen Barad (2007) and Donna Haraway (2016) explicitly reconceptualize empowerment as critical response-ability. That this New Materialist (and post-human) stance, can "flatten human diversity" to miss the experience "of Black, Brown, Latinx, and Indigenous youth and youth from other Subjugated communities, their culture, and epistemologies in everyday interactions, relationships, connections and emotions such as joy and belonging" (Kayumova & Tippins, 2021: 826) is a danger, but others take the Barad/Haraway views as a starting place to conceptualize critical response-ability as a praxis for "the cultivation of collective knowing, desiring, being and making-with so that we render each other capable" (Murris & Bozalek, 2019: 11).

In the work of those highlighting colonial/settler contexts, Édouard Glissant's view of relation seems to be a helpful starting point. In language congruent with Levinas', Glissant claims:

> Relation . . . does not act upon prime elements that are separable or reducible. If this were true, it would itself be reduced to some mechanics capable of being taken apart or reproduced. It does not precede itself in its action and presupposes no *a priori*. It is the boundless effort of the world, to become realized in its totality, that is to evade rest. One does not first enter Relation, as one might enter a religion. One does not first conceive of it the way we have expected to conceive of Being. (Glissant, quoted in King, 2020: 1)

Much analysis of the relationship between Indigenous genocide/settler colonialism and anti-Blackness tends to be prescriptive in that the analysis presumes a certain prescribed politic—whether it be a call for solidarity in a certain way or a call to reject solidarity. But analysis of relationality suggests something otherwise—that the relationality between genocide and anti-Blackness is not fixed and easily knowable.

In other words, relationality cannot be commodification. Scott Pratt's (2002) philosophy of Native American experience is an important source for relocating relation and responsibility in a different key, just as important as the European and later American philosophers I rely on here. Megan Bang et al. (2015) employ critical historicity and transformative agency to incorporate Indigenous perspectives into research methods in education, with a focus on "challenging theories, practices, and structures of values, ethics, and aesthetics—that is, what is good, right, true, and beautiful—that shape current and possible meaning, meaning-making, positioning, and relations in cultural ecologies."

In all cases, responsibility as accountability, as a "disciplinary" term in the Foucauldian sense, is being questioned and/or rejected. The linkage of responsibility to punishment is loosened. Any framing of responsibility that privileges some and not others is discarded, or at least interrogated in an effort to make it possible for more to make and take responsibility.

Unlocking Synergies in Educational Practice

The parallel stories I have told here demonstrate how a focus on responsibility unlocks synergies allowing educators to address multiple educational challenges at the same time. Consider the abiding issues that plague (especially urban) public schools: teacher shortages, inadequate or inappropriate teacher preparation, no career pathways for teachers, inadequate relational capacity in schools, substitute teachers as disruptions, inequitable distribution of resources, school-to-prison-pipeline, and persistently wide disparities in achievement across race and cultural categories. Add in the troubles high on the list today (post-pandemic): "learning loss," mental health and social-emotional support for students, and "right-sizing" technology use.

The educators at Bailey were able to address all of these issues and more because they didn't treat them as discrete problems to be solved. The process of thinking and acting response-ably demands that any "solution" not create new problems.

I am not saying every school should do exactly what was done at Bailey. That is neither possible nor desirable. I am not saying that the kind of response-ability practiced at Bailey will not be found at other schools throughout the world. I am simply saying that response-ability *can* take over even in a public school lacking resources and community support. Finding and developing principals, teachers, specialists, counselors, residents, and paraprofessionals who "get" response-ability—and letting them work—*is* possible. Unfortunately, we have created a bureaucratic system built on prestige and differential compensation by role that encourages educators to move up rather than remain in place to do the challenging and creative work of educating youngsters. We push talented teachers out of the classroom and push accomplished principals to the central office with the mistaken idea that they can tell other people what they have done. This is decidedly not response-ability in action. Addressing these systems is a priority if response-ability can blossom.

Still, the structure is not all that matters. The infrastructure also mattered—the norms, the feelings, the expectations, the habits of interaction and regard fostered by the organic structure that marked teaming at Bailey. So the challenge within districts and schools facing different circumstances and situations from Bailey is to imagine what local structures enable care for teachers so they can maintain a shared and sharp focus on the students. What structures ensure the collaborative teacher autonomy that leads to fluid and just-in-time action in response to the actual needs of students? What structures signal the expansive sense of inclusion that extended to educators no matter what their role and to students no matter what their strengths and needs?

In short, while I am not naïve about the difficulty, I do think that responsibility is a fruitful idea: intrinsically appealing, already in use, and unlocking synergistic thinking. It is not a pipe dream. I might be wrong, of course, but if I am, I am *usefully wrong*. Starting with response-ability opens up energy and resources for enlivening schooling. How that can take shape may be a matter of pragmatist experimentalism.

I conclude with this: a focus on response-ability is both replicable and energizing for educators, and is more generative (with respect to practice, ideas, and affects) than attempting to replicate the abstracted qualities of good schools. Nonetheless, as in all human endeavors, success is elusive.

Afterword: No More Response-ability?

The district announced (in April of 2015, *before* the critical test results were in for 2014–15) that in summer 2016, Bailey would be closed and the students reassigned to a single (remodeled) wing at Stratford High School. District officials could not, perhaps would not, assure Principal Sawyer that he would have *any* job in the district after May 2015 so he sought and found a principal's position in the Denver Public Schools, where he now serves as a director of schools, guiding the principals of twelve other middle schools.

Why was Bailey closed and the students reassigned? Why was Dr. Sawyer's leadership not valued? It is impossible to offer a definitive answer. Based on all I know now, I would say that the die was cast before Dr. Sawyer and the team ever entered the school. The gentrification of East Nashville was pressing hard against the presence in the neighborhood of kids from the projects. Moving the Bailey scholars to Stratford (where their old brothers and sisters were enrolled) made logistical and budgetary sense. It is also true that past failures at Bailey made it very difficult for largely white central administration to imagine even the possibility of educational success, and when it began to appear, they didn't quite believe it. Maybe the transformation just took too long. Under pressure from charter schools hoping to swoop in and a state department of education wanting to take over failing schools, the district administration couldn't make the case to keep Bailey open even in their own minds. In truth, administrators paid more attention to keeping white families in the district than they did to equity and achievement for the least well-off among them, perhaps understandably because those white families were the ones with the political clout to encourage City Council to provide more funding. And c'mon, who really thought a first-time principal could transform the worst school in the state?

Still, in the end, the Bailey team far exceeded the expected measures on both achievement scores and growth scores. The terms of the School Improvement Grant were met. The school rose to solidly satisfactory on the MNPS school performance composite, a measure that combined academic, disciplinary, safety, and satisfaction measures. Despite that success, there would be no reward.

For a year, the teachers and leaders (without Dr. Sawyer but including Dr. Jasper) worked to maintain the Bailey ethos, but systemic factors tilted against them. They began the year with a newly named principal who was in ill health and stalling until he could retire just a few months into the school year. He seemed to know little about what had been happening at Bailey and wanted to know even less. When he went on his final medical leave in October, no one was surprised.

Rather than appoint Dr. Jasper as the interim principal, the district named the assistant principal at Stratford, a long-time and respected educator who was to become the "building principal" for Bailey Middle School when it relocated to Stratford. Given the district's plan, that made sense, but it marked an abrupt shift in culture. The new principal had learned to lead at Stratford. Stratford was a school where directives were issued and expected to be followed. Directives followed meant order, and order was more important than anything.

The relationships between teachers and students persisted, but there were fewer residents to share the load and less attention paid to students' growth and more to following the rules. When the Stratford principal came over to Bailey to "mark it" as his territory, his manner was peremptory and, in truth, alien to the students (who were no longer seen as scholars by their new administration) who had learned to "do school" with Sawyer and Jasper at the helm.

In 2016, after a year in limbo in which teachers and students did their best to maintain the ethos—and performance—that had taken hold, the district closed the school. Just a handful of teachers—and about three-fourths of the students—made the move to Bailey at Stratford. Most of the teachers who did go did not stay at Stratford long. The Bailey experiment in responsibility was over, but response-ability persists in the lives and careers of educators and students who continue, individually and collectively, to reject resignation in the name not of resistance, but of responsibility.

NOTES

Chapter 1

1 All the names associated with Bailey STEM Magnet Middle School are real. All quotes from Bailey staff and scholars are used with permission, taken from personal (recorded) interviews conducted between spring 2021 and fall 2022.
2 I want to make it clear, that in my experience, Dr. Sawyer was not as unusual as he might sound. Most educators know what Sawyer knew—at least until they make the transition from teaching to administration. What makes Sawyer unusual is that he held tight to what his teaching experience and regular encounters with students taught him as he transitioned to the role of principal.
3 The few citations included here have prompted whole lines of thinking that reference response-ability as a linchpin in a naturalistic ethical approach.
4 I acknowledge that my own first introduction to this way of thinking about responsibility, at least theoretically, came from a male Christian ethicist, H. Richard Niebuhr (1963), and one of his interlocutors, Sr. Kathleen Toner, IHM (1977). Neither, however, employed the term "response-ability."
5 Wendy Brown (2017), in *Undoing the Demos*, argues that late capitalism has deformed Western politics beyond recognition. Relatedly, George Saunders suggests in "The Braindead Megaphone" (2007) that political communication is empty but noisy.

6 If you are a reader whose primary interest is teaching and learning, you may choose to sidestep Chapter 2 altogether as just too philosophical in tone and language. Or you may choose to skip over Chapter 2 and even Chapter 3 to get to the concrete enactment of response-ability at Bailey. I will not be offended. Still, I think you'll want to return to those chapters to grab hold of theoretical language to make sense of practice, so that you can explain and defend your own thinking-into-practice.

Chapter 2

1 Legal systems are special cases of this. The "rule of law" involves a socially accepted and acknowledged system that designates more and less serious transgressions of societal norms, specifies processes for determining when those transgressions have in fact occurred, and the assigns consequences for confirmed transgressions. The exercise of response-ability is built in in the creation of the system (through legislation and administration). By social agreement, a system is ordained and those acknowledging that system then accept responsibility for compliance while reserving the right to object conscientiously, to protest elements of the system, and to work for change when that becomes necessary. The fact that there are criminals confirms that some have not taken responsibility for compliance because the system in place does not serve their interests. While some assume that consequences for transgressions constitute punishment—and should, in fact, be punishing—this is not a universal view. In fact, empirical data tends to support the view that harsh punishment is not restorative and often is not even a deterrent.

2 In his *Critical Inquiry* essay defending his relationship with the Nazi sympathizer Paul deMan, Derrida highlights the *aporia* at the center of responsibility that he treats elsewhere.

[R]esponsibility, if there is any, requires the experience of the undecidable . . ., the double edge and the double bind, which are other phenomena of the undecidable. Before answering, responding for oneself, and for that purpose, in order to do so, one must respond, answer to the other, about the other, for the other, not in his place as if in the place of another "proper self," but for him. (Derrida, 1988: 639)

Chapter 3

1 I want to state outright that pragmatism as I employ it here, and practice it philosophically, does not discount the value of careful analytic work, precise phenomenological thinking, deconstruction of meta-narratives, or hermeneutic interpretation. It makes room for these tools as more or less useful depending on the lived challenge and the interpretation that challenge demands. This is broadly evident in the work of William James, Charles Sanders Peirce, and John Dewey, as well as in the work of Jane Addams and Mary Parker Follett.

2 Perhaps the most important point to be made is that the logics and "psychologics" underlying pragmatism align with the logics and psychologics of educational practice.

3 See, for example, Barbara Ehrenreich's 2018 claim, in contradistinction to Barack Obama, that "The arc of history is long, but it bends toward catastrophic annihilation."

4 Cedric Robinson's Black Marxism and Sylvia Winter's Marxist-flavored cultural criticism speak to this question. Robinson asks who could understand democracy's true moral and ethical demands better than those rebellious people farthest from justice. See, for example, https://www.thenation.com/article/society/cedric-robinson-essays/

5 It is worth noting that Dewey addresses this explicitly in Chapter 6 of his classic *Democracy and Education* (2016): "Education as Conservative and Progressive."

6 That struggle played out in the schools is well documented in Ansley Erickson's 2016 book, *Making the Unequal Metropolis*. In a 2020 BET series called "Disrupt and Dismantle," journalist Soledad O'Brien takes up the school-to-prison pipeline in Nashville where high levels of incarceration plague Black neighborhoods and where Black neighborhoods have been systematically held down (by the construction of Route 40) or erased (by focused gentrification).

7 Virtually all moments of habit disruption are uncomfortable, but some are relatively easy to address and even resolve; interpretation and response yield generative options for action. Others, however, are "wicked problems." A wicked problem is a seemingly unique challenge without easy answer or even simple formulation. Wicked problems are typically tied up in other apparently difficult challenges. There is no ultimate test of a solution to a wicked problem; the best one can do is respond so that the situation is better rather than worse—and it is only after an apparent resolution that the problem itself is actually understood. I note this simply to acknowledge that ethical questions of educational practice are not always (easily) answerable.

8 The explicit notion of active open-mindedness can be traced to Jonathan Baron (1991). It is also the defining characteristic of Isaiah Berlin's "fox," distinguishable from the "hedgehog" (1953).

9 As noted earlier, it is common to experience ethical decision-making as something one does individually. And this is accurate as far as it goes. It *is* possible and sometimes certainly desirable to break from the crowd, to act against expectation, to act for oneself. It is also true that when I think through recognition, interpretation, anticipation, and reconstruction, I am directly aware of my own thinking and feeling toward the matter at hand, but have only indirect access to the thoughts and feelings of others. But thinking and feeling are never isolated; the thoughts we think and feelings we feel have arisen and taken shape in interaction with others—even when our decision contradicts those others. Moreover, in settings like Bailey where collaboration is named and welcomed, we are at least aware that we are thinking and feeling *with* others who share some (though perhaps not all) goals, concepts, values, and practices. The point is that ethical thinking and feeling-into-action is always, at its root, an activity that involves "we" and not just "I."

Chapter 4

1 On most measures, Tennessee schools are ranked near the bottom of the list of states. In a recent ranking that discounts achievement and funding, the Heritage Foundation ranks

Tennessee in the Top Ten, largely based on the emphasis on freedom and "choice" available to parents.

2 Race to the Top was an Obama Administration effort to shape states' educational practices by offering substantial federal funding to states who planned reforms that matched Obama's educational priorities. Forty states applied for funding; just two earned the money in the first year. Tennessee was an awardee and granted $500 million dollars. In a state that has approximately a million students in public schools and spends less than $10,000 per student, $500 million dollars is a big bump.

3 I emphasize that these experiments—as all team decisions—were never intended to be permanent fixes but simply responses to a current situation, which would then be reconsidered in time. Just as the teams changed individual scholars' group placements as social, personal, and curricular circumstances demanded, so too did single-sex grouping make sense *under the circumstances*. As circumstances changed (typically after a few weeks), the teams shifted the configuration of scholars. But the decision to employ single-sex instruction temporarily on some teams served the purpose of resetting instruction and allowing the teachers to bring male and female students together again later in productive ways.

4 Too often school districts discourage recommendations for special services assessments because such decisions can have significant budgetary impacts. Sometimes parents are hesitant to label their child, worried that the stigma might outweigh the benefit of the services provided. At all times, the process takes time and effort.

5 Though now defunct after nearly three decades, the Coalition of Essential Schools maintains a website at http://essentialschools.org.

6 Had I not had the Bailey experience and the Bailey team readily available to me, I might well have opted for Central Park East High School as an example of a school where response-ability served as a design principle, a pedagogical guide, and a motivating goal for students.

Chapter 5

1 It is worth noting that every Bailey-affiliated person I interviewed insisted that Bailey was a good school, though their explanations for why varied.

2 See Berliner & Biddle, *The Manufactured Crisis*, 1996. See also annual Phi Delta *Kappan* surveys that demonstrate that Americans give high marks to their own schools, while failing schools generally, a curious phenomenon that is likely linked to the ungrounded school failure rhetoric Berliner and Biddle highlight.

3 N.B. This is a pseudonym, the only name of a Bailey-associated actor that has been changed.

4 See Stengel (2017) for an explanation of critical pragmatist optimism.

5 See Santoro, *Demoralized*, 2018. Santoro captures the affective dynamics that are chasing excellent teachers away from the profession because of lost moral motivation.

REFERENCES

Addams, J. (1907), "Newer Ideals of Peace," excerpted in L. Harris, S. Pratt, & A. Waters (eds), *American Philosophies: An Anthropology*, 389–404, Malten, MA: Blackwell.

Ahmed, S. (2003), *The Cultural Politics of Emotion*, New York: Routledge.

Applebaum, B. (2022), *White Educators Negotiating Complicity: Roadblocks Paved with Good Intentions*, Lanham, MD: Lexington Books.

Arendt, H. (1954/2006), "Chapter 5: The Crisis in Education," in Jerome Kohn (ed), *Between Past and Future*, 170–193, New York: Penguin Classics.

Arendt, H. (2021), *Thinking without a Bannister: Essays in Understanding 1953–1976*, ed. J. Kohn, New York: Random House.

Aristotle. (1985), *Nicomachean Ethics*, trans. T. Irwin, Indianapolis, IN: Hackett Publishing.

Bakewell, S. (2016), *At the Existentialist Café*, New York: Other Press.

Baldwin, J. (1963, December 21), "A Talk to Teachers," *The Saturday Review*, 42–44.

Bang, M., Faber, L., Gurneau, J., Marin, A., & Soto, C. (2015), "Community-Based Design Research: Learning Across Generations and Strategic Transformations of Institutional Relations Toward Axiological Innovations," *Mind, Culture, and Activity*, 23(1): 28–41.

Barad, K. (2007), *Meeting the Universe Halfway*, Durham, NC: Duke University Press.

Barad, K. (2012), "Intra-actions," Interview of Karen Barad by Adam Kleinmann, *Mousse Magazine*, 34: 76–81.

Baron, J. (1991), "Beliefs about Thinking," in J.F. Voss, D.N. Perkins, & J.W. Segal (eds), *Informal Reasoning and Education*, 169–186, Hillsdale, NJ: Erlbaum.

Berlin, I. (1953), *The Hedgehog and the Fox*, London: Weidenfeld and Nicholson.

Berliner, D., & Biddle, B. (1996), *The Manufactured Crisis: Myths, Fraud, and the Attack on America's Public School*, New York: Basic Books.

Blum, L. (2022 Edition, Winter), "Iris Murdoch," in E. Zalta & U. Nodelman (eds), *Stanford Encyclopedia of Philosophy*. Available at https://plato.stanford.edu/archives/win2022/entries/murdoch.

Boler, M. (1999), *Feeling Power: Emotions and Education*, New York: Routledge.

Brown, W. (2017), *Undoing the Demos: Neoliberalism's Stealth Revolution*, Princeton, NJ: Zone Books.

Burke, K., & Greteman, A. (2022), *On Liking the Other: Queer Subjects & Religious Discourse*, Gorham, ME: Myers Education Press.

Cannon, K. (2006), *Black Womanist Ethics*, Eugene, OR: Wipf & Stock.

Chen, G.A., Marshall, S.A., & Horn, I.S. (2020), "'How Do I Choose?': Mathematics Teachers' Sensemaking about Pedagogical Responsibility," *Pedagogy, Culture & Society*, 29(3): 379–396.

Cole, T. (2021), *Black Paper: Writing in a Dark Time*, Chicago, IL: University of Chicago Press.

Collins, P.H. (1990), *Black Feminist Thought: Knowledge, Consciousness, and the Politics of Empowerment*, Oxfordshire: Routledge.

Cooper, A.J. (1892/2017), *A Voice from the South*, Chapel Hill, NC: University of North Carolina Press.

Cottom, T.M. (2022, November 1), "In the Political Talk Show Race, Outrage Is Winning," *New York Times*.

Darling-Hammond, L. (2000), "Solving the Dilemmas of Teaching Supply, Demand, and Standards: How We Can Ensure a Competent, Caring, and Qualified Teacher for Every Child," National Commission on Teaching and America's Future, ED 463337. Available at https://eric.ed.gov/?id=ED463337.

deBeauvoir, S. (1949), *The Ethics of Ambiguity*, trans. B. Frechtman, New York: Philosophical Library.

deBeauvoir, S. (1953), *The Second Sex*, trans. H.M. Parshley, New York: Knopf.

Derrida, J. (1988), "Like the Sound of the Sea Deep within a Shell: Paul de Man's War," trans. P. Kamuf, *Critical Inquiry*, 14(3): 590–652.

Dewey, J. (1891/1976), "Outlines of a Critical Theory of Ethics," in J. Boydston (ed), *The Early Works of John Dewey 1882–1898*, vol. 3, 237–388, Carbondale: Southern Illinois University Press.

Dewey, J. (1894/1976), "The Theory of Emotion. (I) Emotional Attitudes," in J. Boydston (ed), *The Early Works of John Dewey 1882–1898*, vol. 4, 152–169, Carbondale: Southern Illinois University Press.

Dewey, J. (1895/1976), "The Theory of Emotion. (II) The Significance of Emotions," in J. Boydston (ed), *The Early Works of John Dewey 1882–1898*, vol. 4, 170–188, Carbondale: Southern Illinois University Press.

Dewey, J. (1910/1980), "*How We Think*," in J. Boydston (ed), *The Middle Works of John Dewey, 1899–1924*, vol. 6, 178–357, Carbondale: Southern Illinois University Press.

Dewey, J. (1916/1980), "*Democracy and Education*," in J. Boydston (ed), *The Middle Works of John Dewey, 1899–1924*, vol. 9, 3–370, Carbondale: Southern Illinois University Press.

Dewey, J. (1922/1980), "*Human Nature and Conduct*," in J. Boydston (ed), *The Middle Works of John Dewey, 1899–1924*, vol. 14, 3–230, Carbondale: Southern Illinois University Press.

Dewey, J. (1932/1981), "*Ethics*," in J. Boydston (ed), *The Later Works of John Dewey, 1925–1953*, vol. 7, 5–462, Carbondale: Southern Illinois University Press.

Ehrenreich, B. (2018), *Natural Causes: An Epidemic of Wellness, the Certainty of Dying, and Killing Ourselves to Live Longer*, New York: Twelve Books.

Erikson, Ansley. (2016), *Making the Unequal Metropolis*, Chicago, IL: University of Chicago Press.

Follett, M.P. (1995), *The Prophet of Management*, ed. P. Graham, Boston, MA: Harvard Business Press.

Gadamer, H.G. (1998), *Truth and Method*, 2nd rev. ed., trans. J. Weinsheimer & D. Marshall, New York: Continuum.

Gilligan, C. (1982), *In a Different Voice*, Cambridge, MA: Harvard University Press.

Gunzenhauser, M. (2012), *The Active/Ethical Profession: A Framework for Responsible Educators*, New York: Continuum.
Haraway, D. (2016), *Staying with the Trouble: Making Kin in the Chthulucene*, Durham, NC: Duke University Press.
hooks, b. (1994), *Teaching to Transgress*, New York: Routledge.
Joldersma, C. (2014), *Levinasian Ethics for Education's Commonplaces: Between Calling and Inspiration*, New York: Palgrave Macmillan.
Kant, I. (1784/1995), "What is Enlightenment?" in M. Perry et al. (eds), *Sources of the Western Tradition*, vol. II, 56–57, Boston, MA: Houghton Mifflin Company.
Kayumova, S., & Tippins, D. (2021), "The Quest for Sustainable Futures: Designing Transformative Learning Spaces with Multilingual Black, Brown, and Latinx Young People Through Critical Response-ability," *Cultural Studies of Science Education*, 16: 821–839.
Kerdeman, D. (2019), "Pulled Up Short: Exposing White Privilege," in A. Chinnery (ed), *Philosophy of Education 2017*, 1–18, Urbana, IL: Philosophy of Education Society. Available at https://educationjournal.web.illinois.edu/ojs/index.php/pes/article/view/51/20.
King, T.L., Navarro, J., & Smith, A. (2020), *Otherwise Worlds: Against Settler Colonialism and Anti-Blackness*, Durham, NC: Duke University Press.
Kinnell, G. (1989), "The Simple Acts of Life," The Power of the Word with Bill Moyers: A Six-Part Series of Contemporary Poetry, New York: PBS VIDEO, David Grubin Productions.
Kohn, A. (1993), *Punished by Rewards*, Boston, MA: Houghton Mifflin.
Kuokkanen, R. (2007), *Reshaping the University: Responsibility, Indigenous Epistemes, and the Logic of the Gift*, Vancouver: UBC Press.
Labaree, D. (2010), *Someone Has to Fail*, Cambridge, MA: Harvard University Press.
Levinas, E. (1985), *Ethics and Infinity*, trans. R. Cohen, Pittsburgh, PA: Duquesne University Press.
Lipscomb, B. (2022), *The Women are Up to Something: How Elizabeth Anscombe, Philippa Foot, Mary Midgley, and Iris Murdoch Revolutionized Ethics*, Oxford: Oxford University Press.

Lorde, A. (1984), *Sister Outsider*, New York: Penguin.
Mann, H. (1848/2013), "Twelfth Annual Report of Horace Mann as Secretary of Massachusetts State Board of Education," Commonwealth of Massachusetts, Board of Education. Available at https://archives.lib.state.ma.us/handle/2452/204731.
Meier, D. (1995), *The Power of Their Ideas*, Boston, MA: Beacon Press.
Menand, L. (2014, March 17), "The deMan Case: Does a Critic's Past Explain His Criticism?" *The New Yorker*.
Murdoch, I. (1970), *The Sovereignty of Good*, New York: Routledge Classics.
Murris, K., & Bozalek, V. (2019), "Diffraction and Response-able Reading of Texts: The Relational Ontologies of Barad and Deleuze," *International Journal of Qualitative Studies in Education*, 32(1): 1–15.
National Council for Social Studies. (2013), *College, Career, and Civic Life (C3) Framework for Social Studies State Standards: Guidance for Enhancing the Rigor of K-12 Civics, Economics, Geography, and History*. Available at https://www.socialstudies.org/system/files/2022/c3-framework-for-social-studies-rev0617.2.pdf.
Niebuhr, H.R. (1963), *The Responsible Self*, New York: Harper and Row.
Nietzsche, F. (1901/1967), *The Will to Power*, trans. W. Kaufmann & R.J. Hollingdale, ed. W. Kaufmann, New York: Vintage.
Nietzsche, F. (1974), *The Gay Science*, trans. W. Kaufman, New York: Vintage.
Nietzsche, F. (1979), *On Truth and Lies in a Nonmoral Sense*, trans. D. Brazeale, Atlantic Highlands, NJ: Humanities Press.
Nietzsche, F. (1996), *Human, All Too Human*, eds. R. Schacht & R. Hollingdale, New York: Cambridge University Press.
Noddings, N. (1983/2013), *Caring: A Relational Approach to Ethics and Education*, 2nd ed., Berkeley, CA: University of California Press.
Noddings, N. (1993/2005), *The Challenge to Care in Schools*, New York: Teachers College Press.
Oliver, K. (2018), *Response Ethics*, Lanham, MD: Rowman and Littlefield.
Pappas, G. (2018), "What Is Going On? Where Do We Go from Here? Should the Souls of White Folks Be Saved?" *The Pluralist*, 13(1): 67–80.

Peirce, C.S. (2006), "The Fixation of Belief," in S. Haack (ed), *Pragmatism Old and New*, 107–126, Amherst, NY: Prometheus Books.

Pratt, S. (2002), *Native Pragmatism: Rethinking the Roots of American Philosophy*, Bloomington, IN: Indiana University Press.

Raffoul, F. (2010), *Origins of Responsibility*, Bloomington, IN: Indiana University Press.

Santoro, D. (2018), *Demoralized: Why Teachers Leave the Profession They Love and How They Can Stay*, Boston, MA: Harvard Education Press.

Sartre, J.P. (1992), *Being and Nothingness*, trans. H. Barnes, New York: Washington Square Press.

Saunders, G. (2007), "'The New Mecca,' (21–56) and 'The Braindead Megaphone', (1–20)," in *The Braindead Megaphone: Essays*, New York: Riverhead Books.

Saunders, G. (2022, November 8), "Transcript: Ezra Klein Interviews George Saunders," *New York Times*. Available at https://www.nytimes.com/2022/11/08/podcasts/ezra-klein-interviews-george-saunders.html.

Stengel, B. (1999, October), "Pedagogical Response-ability: Dewey and Buber Lay the Ground Work," *Philosophy Studies in Education* (1999): 147–162.

Stengel, B. (2001), "Teaching in Response," in S. Rice (ed), *Philosophy of Education 2001*, 349–357, Urbana, IL: Philosophy of Education Society. Available at https://educationjournal.web.illinois.edu/archive/index.php/pes/article/view/1917.pdf.

Stengel, B. (2017), "From the Editor: Staying Alive," *Educational Theory*, 67(2): 123–129.

Stengel, B., & Casey, M. (2013), "Moral Perception and Pedagogical Responsibility," in H. Sockett & R. Boostrom (eds), *NSSE Yearbook: A Moral Critique of American Education*, 116–135, New York: Teachers College Press.

Stitzlein, S. (2017), *American Public Education and the Responsibility of its Citizens*, Oxford: Oxford University Press.

Toner, K. (1977), *A Critical Analysis of the Concept of Responsible Moral Agency as Found in the Writings of H. Richard Niebuhr*, Unpublished doctoral dissertation, The Catholic University of America.

Townes, E. (2006), *Womanist Ethics and the Cultural Production of Evil*, New York: Palgrave Macmillan Press.
Tyack, D., & Hansot, E. (1981, Summer), "Conflict and Consensus in American Public Education," *Daedalus*, 110(3): 1–25.
Wynter, S. (2022), *We Must Learn to Sit Down Together and Talk about a Little Culture: Decolonizing Essays, 1967–1984*, ed. D.L. Eudell, Leeds: Peepal Tree Press.

INDEX